Leading
With Inquiry
&Action

How Principals Improve
Teaching and Learning

Matthew Militello | Sharon F. Rallis | Ellen B. Goldring
Foreword by Richard F. Elmore

CORWIN
A SAGE Company

For information:

Corwin
A SAGE Company
2455 Teller Road
Thousand Oaks, California 91320
(800) 233-9936
Fax: (800) 417-2466
www.corwinpress.com

SAGE Ltd.
1 Oliver's Yard
55 City Road
London EC1Y 1SP
United Kingdom

SAGE India Pvt. Ltd.
B 1/I 1 Mohan Cooperative
  Industrial Area
Mathura Road, New Delhi 110 044
India

SAGE Asia-Pacific Pte. Ltd.
33 Pekin Street #02-01
Far East Square
Singapore 048763

Library of Congress Cataloging-in-Publication Data

Militello, Matthew.
Leading with inquiry and action : how principals improve teaching and learning / Matthew Militello, Sharon F. Rallis, and Ellen B. Goldring ; foreword by Richard F. Elmore.
    p. cm.
Includes bibliographical references and index.
ISBN 978-1-4129-6413-5 (cloth)
ISBN 978-1-4129-6414-2 (pbk.)

  1. School principals—United States. 2. Action research in education—United States.
I. Rallis, Sharon F. II. Goldring, Ellen B. (Ellen Borish), 1957– III. Title.

LB2831.92.M54 2009
371.2′012—dc22   2009008699

09   10   11   12   13   10   9   8   7   6   5   4   3   2   1

Acquisitions Editor:	Debra Stollenwerk
Associate Editor:	Julie McNall
Production Editor:	Jane Haenel
Copy Editor:	Kathy Pompy
Typesetter:	C&M Digitals (P) Ltd.
Proofreader:	Carole Quandt
Indexer:	Kirsten Kite
Cover Designer:	Lisa Riley

Contents

Foreword

This book gives depth and substance to the *practice* of the principalship. In this sense, it challenges at least two of the most deeply rooted cultural norms around school leadership in the American context. The first of these norms is the idea that leadership grows out of the particular attributes and talents of the individual leader rather than out of learned behavior or practice. The second of these norms is that all leadership is contextual and contingent—that successful leaders in one context are often not likely to be successful in another because their particular "style" of leadership may not be compatible with the new setting. These norms are both deeply rooted in the culture of leadership in American schools and deeply destructive to the creation of a professional culture in schools. If all that is successful about leadership can be explained by the attributes of the individual and their consistency or inconsistency with context, then nothing of any consequence is teachable or trainable, and therefore, there is no such thing as professional knowledge in the sector. Juxtaposed to this view, the authors of this book argue that there is a practice of leadership, or maybe multiple practices of leadership, of which theirs is one and that they can be taught and learned, and indeed, that the practice of leadership itself entails teaching others how to master the complexities of practice in a disciplined and purposeful way. The authors walk us through a process based on a set of fairly widely established practices that revolve around inquiry that connect the major elements of leadership practice to the improvement of instructional practice.

Historians of education have observed that every generation of American educational leaders, from the end of the 19th century onward, promises that *it* will be the generation to transform the practice of leadership into the practice of instructional improvement, and so far, every succeeding generation has failed at that fundamental task. The leadership of instructional practice has been consistently and systematically displaced, generation after generation, by the bureaucratic demands of "running" schools and by the "real-world" demands of school bureaucracy.

This phenomenon has given rise to the wry observation that "educational leadership is to leadership as military music is to music." How is it possible that an aspiration so straightforward and so apparent can consistently be subverted by one generation after another? The answer, I think, lies in the basic observation that education is a profession without a practice or, more accurately, an occupation aspiring to be a profession that has not yet discovered its practice. We do not, as a field, define a set of practices that everyone who enters the sector has to master as a condition of being able to practice, nor do we insist that people who practice in the field continue to learn their practice at ever-increasing levels of competence and expertise over time. This is one of the costs of defining teaching and leadership practices as idiosyncratic attributes of the individual rather than as predictable patterns of behavior that must be learned and developed as a condition of working in the sector.

This book is one of a number of new books on leadership that takes its point of departure from the assumption that there are practices that can be learned, that they can be connected to the core work of schools, and that competence in these practices should be expected of anyone who pretends to the role of "leader" in the sector. The book makes no concessions to the complexity of the work. The first chapter describes the working environment of the principal with uncompromising detail. But rather than taking the traditional route of saying that the work requires extraordinary people with extraordinary talents or, as so often happens in books about educational leadership, arguing that the work is impossible, the book then proceeds, in succeeding chapters, to demonstrate that complex problems require clear, unflinching practices. In this sense, it is a refreshing alternative to the long laundry lists of attributes of successful leaders that pass for guidance to principals in the more traditional literature. The problem with attribute-based leadership theories is that *no one* ever has all the "laundry list" attributes in quite the right combination or quantity and most people don't know how to acquire them if they don't have them. This book argues that educational leadership is—hold onto your hats—about learning, both in the sense of enabling and supporting the learning of teachers and students in classrooms, and in the sense of managing one's own learning as a leader, through collective inquiry with others. Yes, the world of schools is complex. Yes, the work of educational leaders is often difficult, indeterminate, and lonely. But saying that these are the initial conditions of the work only sets the problem. The problem requires a *practice* that breaks the traditional constraints on the learning of adults and children in schools.

Those of us who find ourselves routinely in classrooms and schools know that the culture that constrains learning in schools is more robust and resilient, at least so far, than our best attempts to dislodge it. The authors of this book present a set of ideas and practices that can be used to break the lock of that culture and to transform it into a culture of individual and organizational learning. But these ideas will not affect the lives of educators and children unless the people who work in schools commit themselves to master the practices of transformation in books like this. Exhortations, evidence, and arguments from outside experts will not amount to much if practitioners don't take responsibility themselves for building the professional knowledge and the culture of learning in the sector. The knowledge required to transform the sector has to reside *within schools and school systems* and *within the practice* of people who work in the field, not solely in work of researchers, consultants, and facilitators. The success of research, knowledge development, and consultation around school improvement depends on a steady supply of powerful ideas coming from the field to keep it alive. So this book should be read not only as a source of guidance for practice but also as a provocation to the field to develop *better* ways of doing the work this book describes. Just as in a powerful classroom, the real learning takes place when the teacher releases control over learning and locates it with students; so too will the real learning in this sector take place when the policy makers and experts incite and support practitioners to develop the knowledge that is required to build good research and practice.

Richard F. Elmore
Gregory Anrig Professor of Educational Leadership
Harvard Graduate School of Education

January 2009

Preface

Social, economic, and political forces are driving the calls for change. Once again the burden to innovate and implement the changes has fallen on our schools. Meaningful educational changes must ultimately occur in classrooms. School leaders play an important role in buffering teachers from external forces; at the same time, they press for improved instructional practices. In today's vernacular, this has been labeled as instructional leadership. In this book, we expand the image of instructional leadership to include inquiry and action. We present the *inquiry-minded, action-oriented principal*.

The danger of creating a new image is in replacing one set of jargon with another. Our challenge is to go beyond describing the general and the obvious to uncover what an *inquiry-minded, action-oriented principal* looks like in practice. We introduce Lee, who represents a real-life principal placed in an all-too-common situation. We map Lee's journey using a *collaborative inquiry-action cycle* to operationalize the image of an *inquiry-minded, action-oriented principal*.

We have chosen to make teaching and learning our focus because the core of any school improvement effort is instructional improvement. The business of schooling is teaching and learning; if change does not happen in the classroom, it is not happening at all. Thus, Lee's efforts are directed toward what teachers do in classroom.

WHO MIGHT USE THIS BOOK

The framework and concrete examples we present in this book can be of practical use for school leaders. You may have picked up this book for any of the following reasons:

- You may be a *current principal*, hungry for new strategies to work with your teachers to bring about necessary changes in their classrooms. This book provides a process for engaging your school community in both inquiry and action to bring about the improvements in learning that you seek.

- You may be an *aspiring principal* who is curious about what it looks like to be an effective school leader. This book provides both pictures of an effective principal in practice, as well as the skills, knowledge, and disposition you'll need to become such a leader.
- You may be a *district leader* or a *state policy maker* pressed to raise student achievement outcomes. For district leaders, this book provides a ready-made professional development series for your principals. For state policy makers, this book can serve as a basis for dialogue with district leaders who struggle to meet the achievement mandates.
- You, like us, may be *professors* and/or *professional developers* of all the groups noted above. As teachers of aspiring school principals, we find that current school principals are hungry for tools of change, as are district leaders and policy makers who aim to foster systemic change. We wrote this book to facilitate our work with these groups. We hope that you will also find value in using it in your work.

In addition, we believe that all school personnel can find the content of our example chapters to be useful because we anchor the framework in the hot-button issues of curriculum, assessment, and instruction. For example, Chapter 4 explicates a case of how schools can use data.

WHO WE ARE

Our professional experiences as practitioners, professors, and policy makers have informed this book. Specifically, Lee, our principal protagonist, emerges from the years two of us spent as K–12 school principals and the research that all three of us conduct in schools. The *collaborative inquiry-action cycle* and the illustrative examples are products of our research in schools, our evaluations of educational programs, and our years of K–12 classroom teaching experiences. Our years as professors working with practicing and aspiring principals and policy makers have added to our knowledge and understanding of how schools work and the changing pressures they are under. Our work with the national and state departments of education and professional organizations, as well as local school boards, expands our perspectives. Two of us have watched our children's passage through the public school system; the other is currently watching his children in the process. We have each lived in, around, and with schools our entire lives—we know schools. The result is a book that describes and illustrates the means to become an *inquiry-minded, action-oriented principal*.

HOW WE ORGANIZED THE BOOK

The book is divided into three sections: *From Challenges to Possibilities, The Collaborative Inquiry-Action Cycle in Action,* and *Making It Happen*. We set the stage in Chapters 1 and 2, first identifying the forces that challenge current school improvement efforts. Chapter 1 also summarizes the current literature on school leadership, specifically exploring the *myth of the great principal*. In Chapter 2, we offer a framework with possibilities to meet these challenges—the *collaborative inquiry-action cycle*.

The next three chapters illustrate the cycle in practice, with three independent yet connected examples. Chapter 3's example addresses *a case of curricular alignment*. Chapter 4 provides *a case of data informing practice*. Chapter 5 demonstrates *a case of changing instructional practice*. These cases, with charts, inventories, rubrics, and illustrations, provide models of how the cycle can actually be used in real schools.

The last two chapters make up the *Making It Happen* section. Chapter 6 looks across the three cases and offers analytic insights into *what roles* the principal takes on to enact the collaborative inquiry-action cycle. Finally, in the last chapter, we put Lee and the cycle to the reality test. We ask *does it really work?* We reflect on and evaluate the *collaborative inquiry-action cycle* in practice.

Each chapter begins with a vignette of our principal Lee. The vignettes capture Lee's hopes and anxieties concerning an experience that should be real to readers. From Lee, our middle school principal, we learn what it feels and looks like to be an *inquiry-minded, action-oriented principal*. Lee's actions in the concrete examples illustrate the framework and process amidst the current educational context. This glimpse of Lee's professional life offers insights into the ways the principal responds to and uses new and complex forces that carry demands and expectations for schools and school leaders. Because Lee is a composite of the various school principals we know, have been, and have seen, we recognize that this leader may appear larger than life. Lee's every thought and action, however, derives from at least one practicing principal from our experiences.

We hope that our framing of school improvement and leadership, as well as the examples of Lee in action, will stimulate and provoke further thought. At the end of each chapter, we supply questions and exercises to guide both individual reflection and group discussion. Various audiences may adapt these questions to fit their specific settings, interests, and needs.

Acknowledgments

Past principals we knew, the current principals we teach and collaborate with, and the aspiring principals we are currently preparing—all have inspired us. Among them we have found interactions with the following individuals to be particularly memorable: Steve Baum, Kate England, Michel Fredette, John Goldner, Lora Hall, Jesus Jara, Roland Joyal, Jerry Klomparens, Jon Manier, Darwin Mason, Anne McKenzie, Cheri Meier, Edye Morris-Bryant, Phyliss Schmidt, Muriel Summers, and Thomas Ward. We also acknowledge superintendents who have made space for their principals to become *inquiry-mined, action-oriented principals,* including Mary Conway, Sal Corda, Jake Eberwein, Betty Feser, David Fultz, Fran Gougeon, Bob Janson, Doris Kurtz, Mike McKee, Ronald Militello, Charles Muncatchy, Pat Proctor, Diane Ullman, and Bob Villanova.

We also want to acknowledge our academic and professional colleagues with whom we have worked and dialogued: Maenette Benham, Mark Berends, Kathy Cook, Richard Elmore, Francisco and Miguel Guajardo, Chris Janson, Andrew Lachman, Margaret McMullen, Gretchen Rossman, Richard Ryzenga, Gary Sykes, and Jane Tedder.

We thank our research associates Andrew Churchill, Ian Martin, and Liz Militello for their hours of searching and editing. The graphics would not have been possible without the skills of Jason Schweid and John Militello, who was also the artistic inspiration behind the book cover. We are grateful to two doctoral-level classes, one in school leadership and the other in organizational change, who read and ripped apart our earliest drafts of the book.

Finally, we acknowledge those from whom we have learned the most regarding learning, teaching, and educating America's youth, our children: Bethany (former high school Latin teacher and aspiring psychologist), Ariel (college senior and aspiring policy advisor), Oren (college sophomore and aspiring wilderness therapist), Dominic (seventh grader and aspiring Ferrari and Lamborghini owner), Luke (fourth grader and aspiring cheetah conservationist), and Gabriel (first grader and aspiring Jedi Knight).

PUBLISHER'S ACKNOWLEDGMENTS

Corwin gratefully acknowledges the contributions of the following reviewers:

Russ Bennett
Superintendent
Aurora City Schools
Aurora, OH

Judy Brunner
Author, Consultant, University Faculty
Instructional Solutions Group & Missouri State University
Springfield, MO

Cynthia Church
Principal
Black Hawk Elementary School, Marquardt School District 15
Glendale Heights, IL

Bruce Deterding
Principal
Wichita Heights High School
Wichita, KS

Dr. Brenda S. Dietrich
Superintendent
Auburn-Washburn School District
Topeka, KS

Dr. Marie Kraska
Professor
Auburn University
Auburn University, AL

Patricia M. Richardson, PhD
Professor of Practice, Educational Leadership
University of Maryland
College Park, MD

About the Authors

Matthew Militello is an assistant professor in the Educational Policy and Leadership Studies Department at North Carolina State University. He held a similar position at the University of Massachusetts, Amherst, where he was also the educational administration program coordinator. Prior to his academic career, Militello was a middle and high school teacher, assistant principal, and principal in Michigan. His research focuses on developing principals' knowledge and skills in the areas of school law, school data, and collective leadership. He has led a number of research teams, including the development of professional standards and corresponding key practices for school principals, a statewide study of the validity, implementation, and use of formative assessments systems in school districts, a national study of exemplary high school leadership practices, and a study of principals' professional development needs in Northwest China. Militello has more than 25 publications, including articles in *Education and Urban Society, Harvard Educational Review, Journal of Research on Leadership Education, Journal of School Leadership, Principal Leadership*, and *Qualitative Inquiry*. He received his undergraduate degree and teaching certification from the University of Michigan and his master of education and PhD from Michigan State University.

Sharon F. Rallis is the Dwight W. Allen Distinguished Professor of Education Policy and Reform at the University of Massachusetts, Amherst, where she is also director of the Center for Education Policy. A past-president of the American Evaluation Association, Rallis has been involved with education and evaluation for over three decades. She has been a teacher, counselor, principal, researcher, program evaluator, director of a major federal school reform initiative, and an elected school board member. She has also been professor of education at the University of Connecticut, lecturer on education at Harvard, and associate professor of educational leadership at Peabody College, Vanderbilt University. Currently, her teaching includes courses on inquiry, program evaluation, qualitative methodology, and organizational theory. Her research has focused on the local implementation of programs driven by federal, state, or district policies. She is currently studying alternative training and professional development programs for leaders. Her doctorate is from the Harvard Graduate School of Education. Other Corwin books she has coauthored include *Principals of Dynamic Schools: Taking Charge of Change*; *Dynamic Teachers: Leaders of Change*; and *Leading Dynamic Schools: How to Create and Implement Ethical Policies*.

Ellen B. Goldring is a professor of education policy and leadership at Peabody College of Vanderbilt University, where she won the Alexander Heard Distinguished Professor Award. Her areas of expertise and research focus on improving schools, with particular attention to educational leadership and access and equity in schools of choice. She is the immediate past coeditor of *Educational Evaluation and Policy Analysis*. She serves on numerous editorial boards, technical panels, and policy forums and is the coauthor of four books, including *Leading With Data* (Corwin), as well as hundreds of book chapters and articles. Goldring is currently working on a project funded by the Wallace Foundation to develop and field-test an education leadership assessment system and establish its psychometric properties. She is also conducting experiments to study professional development and performance feedback for school leaders. She is an investigator at the National Center on School Choice and the Learning Sciences Institute at Vanderbilt. Goldring received her PhD from the University of Chicago.

PART I

From Challenges to Possibilities

The Myth of the Great Principal

Lee stared at the door as Fran, the superintendent of the small urban district, left the principal's office in Horizon Elementary School. Lee was not sure whether to feel excited or sad—or just plain scared.

"Phew, he wants me to take over Marshall Middle. This will be my third principalship—first Vibrant Springs, then Horizon for five years, now another. Fran said that because the other two schools are doing so well, he knows I can turn around Marshall. I'm not so sure. Let's face it, both Springs and Horizon have all the components of a dynamic school: teachers who press for instructional improvement, lots of programmatic options for teachers to use with students, a rich and varied and connected curriculum, people willing to act as instructional leaders, parents and a community willing to engage with us in positive and supportive ways. And resources. OK, not a lot of money, but ample materials, lots of energy and willingness to put in time to get things done. The union reps at both schools never took the hard line, like when I wanted the inquiry teams to meet before school."

But Marshall was not Horizon. The superintendent's words rang in Lee's ears "You did a great job at Horizon—you moved the teachers, but more important you moved the students forward. You really knew those kids. You brought the community into the school in meaningful ways that worked—not just parents with their personal agendas and not contrived rhetoric. Bridged that gap between school and the world outside. Now I need you to work your magic at Marshall Middle. I'm behind you all the way." Lee translated his words as "I have a tough assignment for you. You can do it. Good Luck!"

Now Lee was both exhilarated and uncertain. "Can I do it? What is my magic? Grades 6 through 8 are so different. And what do I know about Marshall?" The previous principal, Stan, had been the face of this school for 15 years. Lee had never heard anybody question the operations and teaching practices of Marshall. On the surface, everything seemed straightforward and simple: This middle school's achievement scores were OK, and the school community was silent. Only recently when the state forced the district to look at student achievement data by subgroups did Marshall's image become more complex. The data revealed that several subgroups were below the mastery standard set by the state. Specifically, the African American students were below standard in seventh-grade math and eighth-grade reading, the English language learner (ELL) and many Latino/Latina students were below in seventh-grade reading, and the special education students were well below in all areas.

Reaction to a newspaper article that publicized the scores was swift and extensive. Parents suddenly wanted to know why their children were deficient and what was going to be done. Some, those of traditionally successful kids, considered sending their kids to private schools. The local NAACP chapter wanted a specific action plan detailing how the school would address the inequities across racial groups. At the same time, a school board member campaigned to add a gifted and talented program to the school. Another board member called for a back-to-basics approach. Meanwhile, Marshall's health and art teachers wrote a letter to the editor voicing their concerns that a narrow focus on basics would rob students of a well-rounded educational experience. Teachers complained that class size made it impossible to meet all kids' needs. The assistant superintendent for curriculum issued a memo reminding teachers to adhere to the district curriculum and Pacing Guides. The superintendent charged Stan to develop a school improvement plan that would show results. Stan retired.

Another image of Marshall surfaced from the back of Lee's mind. The district administrative council's meetings rotated around the schools, so Marshall's turn to host the meeting had come during the past year. Lee had been shocked at the climate in the halls—teachers made no eye contact with anyone else, no hellos, no casual conversations; students shuffled listlessly in bunches, no high fives, indolent near-whispered talking. No student work visible. No energy. No connections. No curiosity. Something was wrong. Marshall seemed to be imploding under all the pressures.

Precarious times at Marshall, thought Lee. All the forces are striking at once. But wait. Horizon was not immune to these pressures. How did I deal with everything there? I could have chosen to take command and issue directives. But instead, I remember taking the time to understand what was behind each force and what the various groups wanted. I could not just react to each demand in isolation. Then came the real work—bringing people on board to recognize that we all really want the same thing—to create a place where each kid can learn and grow. Then we acted, working together toward solutions.

Can I do this at Marshall? Yes. I can draw on my Horizon experience and on what I've been learning about successful schools and the principals who run them. One certainty—as principal, I can make a difference.

T he position Lee accepted is typical, challenging, and critical. Lee's job is *typical* because schools are caught in a new era of educational demands. Lee's job is *challenging* because it remains relatively unknown what exactly a principal does to improve student achievement. Lee's job is *critical* because a principal has the most influence on what happens in a school. Therefore, Lee matters. Lee will make a difference at Marshall Middle School, one way or the other.

In this chapter, we identify forces that currently impact schools. Then, we critique the myth of the great principal, choosing not to perpetuate this myth that shapes current practices and policies related to school leadership. Instead, we recognize that the principal does not act alone but operates within a complex interactive environment. Still, the principal matters. So next we offer cases of successful school reform efforts and summarize what is known about how successful principals lead.

FORCES IMPACTING SCHOOLS

The enterprise of schooling would be simple if students were all that teachers and principals had to deal with. But schooling is not that simple. Multiple, complex, compelling—and often competing—internal and external forces demand attention. However, a successful school does not allow these forces to define it. Rather, a successful school harnesses these forces to support the work and outputs that are the core of schooling: *student emotional and cognitive learning.*

The context of setting, population, and the current political and social demands have created ebbs and flows in the enterprise of schooling. Therefore, there is no single prototype of a successful school—they can take many forms. Nevertheless, there are a number of defining features that span content and context boundaries. Rallis and Goldring (2000) identified what they called "dynamic schools" that all exhibited the following characteristics: (1) teachers who press for improvement, (2) programmatic and curricular options, (3) instructional leadership focused on teaching and learning, (4) engaged parents and communities, and (5) the utilization of readily available resources. Horizon was successful because it was a dynamic school; it leveraged the forces to serve children's learning. Lee now needs to learn which forces are in play at Marshall and how Marshall is responding to these forces. Then, Lee can harness the forces to reinvent Marshall as a dynamic school. In this section we describe forces common across today's educational landscape in which all principals work.

Currently schools have to act and react to the following forces:

- Accountability
- Student diversity
- Globalization
- Competition
- Community-district-school relationships

Accountability

Today's educational accountability is, put simply, assessment accountability. Federal accountability via No Child Left Behind (NCLB) has placed heavy weight on outcome assessments. For example, adequate yearly progress (AYP) mandates improvement on standardized state outcome measures. The main source of state outcomes is state-based, NCLB-sanctioned, assessments. Today's accountability is now synonymous with outcome testing of students and the sanctions that accompany the results (Darling-Hammond, 2004; Ogawa, Sandholtz, Martinez-Flores, & Scribner, 2003). Historically, educational sanctions have been directed at the district level. This era of assessment accountability targets the building level—specifically, students, teachers, and principals. Students are targeted in states with high-stakes testing because the assessments are used as a requirement for graduation. The impact on teachers is the public dissemination of classroom assessment results. Principals are sanctioned by threats—placement in a different building or, at worst, losing their jobs.

Often lost in the mire of the sanctions is the possibility for using assessment data to improve instruction for all. Federal and state mandates require schools to report subgroup progress on assessments rather than aggregate scores. Some laud this policy as a new educational rights movement (Skrla, Scheurich, Johnson, & Koschoreck, 2004). That is, it spotlights subgroup achievement gaps that have been previously ignored. The availability of this disaggregated data can encourage educators to make more informed decisions about instructing specific groups of students. The focus on student achievement data moves away from deficit thinking—as Rothstein (2004) stated, "Demography is not destiny" (p. 61). Looking at data can serve to debunk superstitious beliefs about achievement (e.g., family circumstances) (Massell & Goertz, 2002) and can help educators focus on root causes of assessment inequalities rather than on symptoms (Valencia, Valencia, Sloan, & Foley, 2004).

Others see standardized outcome testing as simply an underfunded, superficial policy that has limited impact on student achievement; some even suggest more dangerous impacts as a result of the emphasis on assessment. The expected "huge infusion of new federal funds that would add resources to the schools required to produce large improvements" (Orfield, 2004b, p. 4) was never realized. In the end, schools were told to improve with no additional resources or support but were still held accountable for improving student achievement. This created an over-emphasis on testing without acknowledging the connection among curriculum, instruction, and assessment. Today, the assessment "tail has definitely been wagging the curriculum/instruction canine" (Popham, 2004, p. 420). Research has exposed unintentional consequences of assessment accountability:

- Teaching to the test (Amrein & Berliner, 2002; Carnoy, Loeb, & Smith, 2003; Earl & Katz, 2002; Earl & Torrance, 2000; Haney, 2000; Jones & Egley, 2004; Kornhaber, 2004; Massell, 2001; McNeil, 2000; Popham, 2001)
- Overdepartmentalization as a result of the curricular isolation (Siskin, 2003)
- Steady decline and marginalization of the nontested (e.g. vocational and humanities) courses in schools today (Siskin, 2003)
- Decrease in student efficacy (Black, 2005; Merchant, 2004)

For good or bad, assessment accountability raises the stakes for student performance and has moved the unit of analysis from the community and district level to the school and classroom level (Fuhrman, 1999).

For accountability to improve educational outcomes, certain conditions must exist:

1. An equal focus on instruction and outcomes

2. Authentic use of multiple data sources (including formative assessments and perceptional data) as well as state assessment data

3. Incentives that support instructional innovation balanced with best practices

4. Balance between school-based professional autonomy and reasonable organizational constraints, such as alignment with state-level student learning benchmarks

Student Diversity

Another force with which the principal contends daily inside the school is the diversity of the student body and the variant and pressing needs students bring with them. This diversity carries opportunities as well as challenges. The changing demographics of our nation are evident in our schools' student bodies, which reflect an array of colors, languages, and national heritages. This multicultural cornucopia can provide a rich resource to a school if the principal and teachers can recognize and tap into the riches. Doing so, however, can be a challenge. The school will serve as a primary opportunity for socialization, but as student diversity increases, the task becomes more difficult and the outcome more unpredictable. To provide a just and authentic learning environment, school leaders must be aware of the myriad diversity factors against a background of normative elements within their schools. While traditional conceptions of diversity have focused primarily on race, more nuanced understandings of diversity also take into account economic status, language, able-bodiedness, sexuality, gender identity, and religion.

Race remains the most outward symbol of diversity in American schools. Currently 59% of students in K–12 schools are White, 17% are Black, and 18% are Hispanic (National Center for Educational Statistics [NCES], 2006). By the year 2020, less than half of students in public schools are projected to be White. While this diversity offers both great opportunities and challenges, it is also misleading. For a White student, the average school is composed of almost 80% White students. For a Black or Hispanic student, the school has approximately 60% similar race students (Orfield & Lee, 2005). Dropout rates continue to decline across ethnic groups (more than 10 percentage points from Blacks and Hispanics); nonetheless a substantial gap between groups exists (NCES, 2008; Orfield, 2004a). As such, principals must still address issues commonly associated with 1960s era desegregation; overt and subtle racism, peer integration, systemic oppression, and inequitable expectations.

Beyond racial diversity, socioeconomic diversity is widely acknowledged as a major factor in schools. Today, over 40% of all fourth graders are eligible for free or reduced priced lunch (NCES, 2006). Increasingly researchers and practitioners are identifying social class as a larger predictor of cultural and performance indicators than race (see Rothstein, 2004). Thus, school leaders must deal not only with racial inequities and tensions but also with issues of socioeconomic class.

The racial and economic mix is augmented by the influx of immigrants: students from Southeast Asia, the Caribbean Islands, Latin America, the Middle East, Eastern Europe, and Russia. Currently U.S. public schools house more than 15 ethnic groups with populations greater than 100,000 students. More than 20% of students in public schools speak a language other than English at home, up from 9% in 1979 (NCES, 2008). As a result, rates of students needing English as a second language (ESL) instruction or limited English proficiency (LEP) classes continues to rise. On top of language needs, increasingly large numbers of children come from war-torn countries where they experienced physical and psychological trauma. In all cases, the principal is challenged to bring these children into a safe, nurturing school community where they will be in mainstream classes and assessed on state measures.

Also at play in the lived diversity of schools are issues of able-bodiedness, sexuality, gender identity, and religion. Over 6.5 million students, or 16% of all students, have specific disabilities (NCES, 2006). These students are characterized by differences in learning, emotion, and physicality. Some require extensive medical attention, others require subtle adjustments to lesson planning, and still others receive no services. While legislation has focused considerable amounts of energy on creating equitable spaces for children with disabilities, the same cannot be said for those with differing sexualities and gender identification. These diversity factors also require attention in schools. In 2007, Human Rights Watch, an international nongovernmental organization (NGO) that investigates and reports on war crimes and governmental oppression, cited the U.S. public school system for the prevalence of violence and harassment against gay, lesbian, bisexual, and transgender (GLBT) students and the lack of action from school administrators. The brief cites student, teacher, and administrator violence and harassment.

Students in today's schools worship the pantheon of world religions. While religious diversity and tolerance is guaranteed by the First Amendment, schools have become a testing ground for this right. Beyond court decisions, judgments can be made by community norms, in the hallways and playgrounds, and in instructional choices. With increased media attention to systemic cases of religious intolerance and continuing questions about the role of prayer, evolution, and religious preference in schools, leaders must be aware of the nuances in their school's religious environment.

While current trends in judicial and legislative decision making may aim to simplify conceptions of diversity, diversity is not a simple issue for principals. Principals must not only meet the myriad of needs that this diverse mix of students brings but must also actively work to ensure that past injustices are not replicated. Whatever their needs, these children are in our schools, and to some extent, society looks to the school to meet their needs. Today's conceptions of diversity move beyond tolerance and accommodation to inclusion, acknowledgment, and celebration. The opportunity is to capitalize on each group's contribution to the environment; the challenge is to address the inequities and to reduce the tensions. This requires a special type of leadership. In sum, the awareness of the needs, rights, and contributions of the various groups introduces a vast set of demands and expectations on curricular, as well as extracurricular, offerings and on those who lead the school. Today's principals can view student diversity as a resource for teaching and learning.

Globalization

Thomas Friedman used the "flat world" term to signal how technological advances have created a different kind of world economy and communication system (see Friedman, 2007). While Copernicus fought to prove that our world was *not* flat, Friedman uses the metaphor to demonstrate how the economic and communicative changes in our world are having (or should have) an impact on the traditions of schooling from kindergarten to postsecondary. Specifically, this globalized world has created a new demand for a new economy. Historically, societies have targeted schools to develop the kinds of workers needed to sustain and expand an economy. Countries around the world (Friedman uses India and China as primary examples) have developed national strength through a burgeoning economy. Today, technical skills and English are being taught to workers in these countries. The result has been a steady transition of jobs outside the United States. While such outsourcing has increased consumer buying power in the United States, critics cite the decreasing rate of employment. This outsourcing also raises demand for higher skill-level jobs. As a result, the call to better prepare U.S. students, especially in math and science, has become a *real* pressure in K–12 schooling.

As a consequence, there is a palpable shift in the purpose of education. Labaree (1999) described the purpose of education as (1) democratic equity, (2) social efficiency, and (3) social mobility. Today, schools have the added burden of preparing for survival in a global market. Educational policy and schools have responded with a clearer focus on academic rigor in math and science. Schools have begun to "double-block" core subject courses to the detriment of the arts, physical education, and the humanities (see Siskin, 2003). While obtaining proficiency in core subject areas is not questioned, the need to take into account creativity, innovation, and artisanship continues to be a hallmark of strong economies (see Florida, 2002; Pink, 2006). Rothstein (2004) cites the consistent desire for employers to have workers with basic communication skills and a strong work ethic over specific cognitive skills. Interestingly, Friedman's (2007) most recent version of the flat world cites how countries like Singapore and China are looking for a more holistic educational experience for their children.

While the road to economic success may be paved with proficiency in the core subject areas, sustainability and growth are rooted in striking a balance between core knowledge and creativity and innovation. Today's schools stand as the fulcrum in this debate. Schools not only have to educate all students; they must educate the whole child, affectively and cognitively. Moreover, schools must educate students with a variety of special needs and a diverse set of supports outside the schoolhouse doors. Success in a global or flat world will not hinge on more narrowed and specified curricula. Rather, schools must stick to their holistic mission to teach all children. This will require curricular and pedagogical diversity aimed at fully developing and preparing today's students for tomorrow's world.

Competition

Recent reform policies have attempted to apply market principles to K–12 schools. These policies are framed as offering parents choices among school options for their children (see Chubb & Moe, 1990). One argument for offering choice is that competition among educational providers (for students and resources) will force public schools to improve. Proponents of choice assert that local governments hold monopolies over public education. The inherent lack of competition has "spawned a culture of mediocrity, unresponsiveness, and indifference to student performance. Requiring schools to compete for students and funding . . . will force them to demonstrate their capacity to deliver a quality product in order to survive in a market where parents, as education consumers, can choose to vote with their feet and leave a school with which they are dissatisfied" (Lacireno-Paquet, Holyoke, Moser, & Henig, 2002, pp. 146–147).

Competition or choice encompasses an array of different arrangements, including public vouchers for private and parochial schools, charter schools, interdistrict public school choice, intradistrict public school choice, magnet or desegregation programs, vocational options, special education programs, and homeschooling. In addition, perhaps the most pervasive form of school choice is family selection of particular communities in which to live, based on perceived school quality. Federal and state standards-based reforms have aided in this competitive pressure by making school and district test results more publicly available for comparison.

School choice has been touted as a promising education reform strategy for a range of reasons. Some advocates argue that from an equity standpoint, school choice provides expanded educational opportunities to low-income students, who have been trapped within persistently under-performing schools. Others believe that students' motivation and performance will be greater if families are able to choose the direction of their children's education. Still others assert that choice will lead to better matching of students and schools, thus improving their educational experience. Proponents of market economics believe that the mainstream educational delivery system will become more efficient and effective because increased competition drives innovation and improvement. Many contend that schools that are freed from the constraints of the traditional system will become beacons of learning and laboratories of innovation, developing and sharing new educational ideas. Philosophically and pedagogically, advocates believe that school choice offers hope for expanded educational equity, opportunity, and improvement.

On the other hand, opponents cite concerns that include the demise of the American common school and the potential for further balkanization of public education by ethnicity, race, class, and income. Others criticize vouchers and the 2002 U.S. Supreme Court *Zelman* decision for blurring the separation between church and state. Critics of market-based public education oppose the profiteering of private companies that are engaged in school and district management, while some resent any diversion of funds from mainstream schools. Others warn that people who are most at risk (the poor) will not benefit from a market-based system because they are the least equipped to navigate such a system and may lack the means (e.g., transportation) to participate. Similarly, schools that are most at risk will not benefit from the market-based system because they lack the financial means to advertise and they are viewed as having little to offer and thus cannot compete for students.

Competition from choice options can push mainstream schools in several different directions. On the one hand, schools may respond to, say, a nearby arts-focused charter school by increasing arts-related offerings. On the other hand, funding formulas in which per-student funds "follow the student" often reduce revenues for "sending" schools in significant ways, but reductions in student numbers may not be large enough on a per-classroom basis to enable "sending" schools to realize corresponding cost savings by laying teachers off.

Lubienski (2006) finds that "peculiarities of the public school sector" (p. 324) may keep schools from responding to competition as expected by advocates: (1) Instead of innovating in the classroom, new schools often embrace traditional practices; (2) innovations are often limited to administration and marketing rather than being fostered at the classroom level; and (3) the most innovative and diversified options appear to be produced by public-sector policies rather than by competitive pressures. Principals in schools that are troubled by competition would do well to focus not on attracting new students but rather on providing a rich, rigorous, and meaningful educational experience for students already in their schools.

Community-District-School Relationships

Today's school leaders are being pulled in many different directions by powerful, influential constituencies in their school, district, and community. An effective school leader must maintain balance among these groups through strategic diplomacy and skill (Lutz & Merz, 1992). An influencing force that is often underdeveloped in administrator training is parent and community involvement in schooling (Epstein & Sanders, 2006). The ways in which community members and families interact with the school system are of crucial importance to the overall placement of schools within the community. Based upon this interaction, schools can look different. Some schools maintain a culture of authority and interact with the community formally and traditionally, while others actively seek to define the school as a valuable hub of social and community resources. Both extremes warrant very different approaches and implications for the management of community influence.

In traditional schools, managing the community involves recognizing powerful individuals and groups in the community and maintaining good public relations (i.e., attending the local Lions Club meetings, maintaining a weekly newsletter, participating in an annual food drive, etc.). However, now, more than ever, schools are seen as stable anchors in a tumultuous community setting. Reformers are thus linking schools with their communities in new ways. Many urban cities are combating fragmented social services to children by encouraging schools to join with their communities and collaborate with social service agencies (Mawhinney, 1996). Numerous models are in place that link schools with health and welfare agencies to serve children and their families (Adler & Gardner, 1994; Rothstein, 2004). These new initiatives, aimed at meeting the needs of a wide range of types of children and their families, place new and different demands on the school and the principal as "schools are considering what happens to children beyond the confines of the school" (Goldring & Sullivan, 1996, p. 206). The school is no longer responsible only for educating the child; it is responsible for the total well-being of the child.

But working to create a more "full service" school requires vision and skill beyond the simple management of community influence. Engaging with the community requires intentionally studying the school's capacity to connect school functions to the needs of the community (Rothstein, 2004). Principals are now involved in programs and activities beyond the school curriculum. Schools may expand programs into a noninstructional array of services, and in some cases, they may completely change a school's purpose (Crowson & Boyd, 1993). Whatever their scope, the newly created expectations about the place of schools in the larger community "demands a reorientation for both families and schools to a set of relationships which exceed the tenuous, negotiated parameters demarcating professional and private spheres" (Smrekar, 1993, p. 3). They interact with professionals beyond classroom teachers and guidance counselors. They also work with community leaders to involve students in community work (Eberly, 1993; Militello & Benham, in press).

Many leaders find the broader and complex community outside of their doors overwhelming and the needs of the community too great to address in schools. Despite the obvious difficulties, balancing the influence of the community through intentional programming may ultimately enable a spanning of boundaries as well as providing a natural buffer that protects the school from negative community influence (community dissatisfaction in schools, changes in local politics, voters denying funding, changes in demographics or economic status, or power shifts within the community) (Lutz & Merz, 1992). Therefore, effective leaders understand the long-term benefits of managing influencing factors. They willingly approach interactions with families and community members to address the positive and negative values and attitudes affecting school involvement; they create climates conducive to trusting family, community, and educator relationships; and they design strategies that promote a sense of shared responsibility (Christenson & Sheridan, 2001). While these activities represent a great deal of work and collaboration, they pay dividends through the public value that family and community members place upon the school.

Schools do not exist in a void; they are embedded in the social context of their surrounding communities. The social fabric of society reveals a tapestry of families with diverse structures, employment arrangements, racial and ethnic backgrounds, health care needs, and support systems— all of which have tremendous impact on the school and the principal. Relationships with the multifaceted community place new demands on schools but also make principals pivotal in both meeting demands and in exploiting the resources within.

Summary of Forces

These forces are at work in schools. And there are other forces that exist, some unique to a community and others systemic (e.g., high teacher turnover that is especially chronic in low-income communities). How can principals cope with them? Faced with the challenges these forces bring, the principal has several options: The principal can ignore them—to the peril of the school; the principal can react to them—allowing them to drive the school; or the principal can take charge—using them ethically to shape the school. Principals like Lee do the latter; they use these forces to advance teaching and learning. Often, the burden for dealing with these forces falls primarily on the principal, thus establishing the myth that the principal does all.

THE MYTH OF THE GREAT PRINCIPAL

An effective school requires a manager competent in maintenance functions to insure a positive school climate. A building must run smoothly; activities must be coordinated; students and teachers must feel safe. At the same time, teachers in an effective school require an instructional leader to support their instructional efforts and their professional development. Both maintenance and development are essential components of an effective school, and in most schools, both functions are the duty of a single individual: the building principal. An effective principal has always been expected to keep a school running smoothly; now, current principals are also expected to spend more time as leaders of curriculum, instruction, and assessment.

The job can be overwhelming. Schools are complex organisms that respond to several levels of policy. At the same time, schools react to the immediate context-specific demands of the local community. Agendas vary across constituencies, each describing the purposes, activities, and resources of the school from a singular perspective. The principal may well be the only person in the school who is able to see the whole picture—and to make sense of it. Seldom does anyone other than the principal have access to all the varied systems operating more or less independently in the loosely coupled components of the school (see Weick, 1976). The demands on the principal are heavy and come from wide-ranging sources—from policy makers to local businesspeople to the children in the classrooms. To perform the many tasks of the job, principals need a broad knowledge base and multiple skills. They need to understand children and child development, pedagogy and learning styles, and philosophies of education. They need competence in operations and finance. They need familiarity with their community. They need skill in communication and in techniques for working effectively with adults.

Management alone could fill the principal's days. He or she must orchestrate all the loosely coupled structures of the building organization so that they work together smoothly. Before teachers can begin to instruct students, custodians must prepare classrooms and clean hallways; classes must be scheduled and students assigned; cafeteria workers must prepare meals; heat and electricity must be working; and most of all, there must be continual communication with parents and district offices. Principals manage the building operations by monitoring and coordinating activities so that teachers, students, and parents know what to expect and feel safe. And in fact, these management tasks are what principals are most often held accountable for at the district level.

Arguably the more important responsibility of the principal is that of instructional leader: identifying learning needs, establishing directions for curriculum and instruction, connecting to best practices, using data, and facilitating teachers' learning. Instruction, while still the heart of schooling, is only one of the many arenas for decision making in schools. And recent accountability demands on achievement outcomes have brought instructional leadership to the fore.

Throughout the past decades, numerous commissions, studies, and laws have aimed at improving student achievement by making schools more accountable. For principals this translated into "work harder"— making the burden of an already difficult job even greater. However, organizational structures and resource allocation remain largely unchanged, and teachers still are able to close their doors and do what they want in the classroom (see Lortie, 1975; Tyack & Cuban, 1995). The charge for change falls on school principals; they are the ones expected to generate strategic solutions and lead day-to-day implementation. Moreover, there is little evidence that leadership training, compensation, and support have made notable gains in conjunction with the new demands to achieve the goals set forth by the assessment-accountability movement.

When sanctions are attached to policy and the stakes increase, organizations and their leaders tend to respond in a command style (Rowan, 1990). Administrators have tremendous burdens to comply symbolically (Ogawa et al., 2003) with mandates that may lead to highly centralized behaviors (Lemons, Luschei, & Siskin, 2003). Spillane (2000) characterizes this command style of leadership as behavioristic, where leaders are authoritarian in order to meet the compliance-based mandates of accountability. Specifically, accountability demands evoke a Pavlovian-like response to search for an immediate solution, often choosing the first to appear. This reactive process leads to organizational tunnel vision (Brown & Duguid, 2000; March & Levinthal, 1999) where the chosen alternatives are most often sought in the neighborhood of old ones (DiMaggio & Powell, 1991; March, 1999c). Unfortunately, this process ignores the impact on the overall school environment, inhibits risk taking, inquiry, and conversation among the various players, and often results in the creation of a new set of problems that need an immediate solution. Such an approach is antithetical to building teacher capacity (Elmore, 2003a).

Trapped in this tunnel vision, principals feel isolated. Isolation leads to loneliness. This bureaucratic model sets up a one-way response system. Constituents come to the principal's office dumping their problems and personal details. They do not want to leave without a solution they can be comfortable with. The often dysfunctional, linear nature of this interaction reminds us of the 1990s maxim *garbage in, garbage out*. The pressures on principals to find and implement solutions to poorly defined problems cause them to be reactive, which isolates them further. They are at the center of activity, but they are alone. Their loneliness is strange and disconcerting. Driscoll (2007) notes in Philip Jackson's experience as principal/director of the University of Chicago Laboratory Schools:

> But it is to loneliness that he returns more than once, and to the isolation that school leaders feel on a day-to-day basis, feelings that originate in part from the deep and surprisingly intimate knowledge of the faculty and school community that comes, often unbidden, to those in leadership positions; . . . to know and yet not to be able to share such confidence. (p. 98)

The ambiguity is exacerbated "by the sense that one is under constant surveillance" (Driscoll, 2007, p. 98). Responsible for both vision and management, in the public eye, privy to details both technical and private, and at the same time, isolated within the position, a principal can easily become overwhelmed. However, Spillane (2000) suggests that a "situative" or cognitive leadership approach is more effective to elicit deep teacher change and instructional improvement. Such an approach differs from the command style because it facilitates consideration of what is needed, who contributes, and the work to be done—all to reach an agreed upon goal.

The *Great Principal* is little more than a myth, as both attracting and retaining highly qualified principals has become problematic. The "revolving door" of the principalship has been fueled by pressure and demands that make the job nearly untenable. As Fink and Brayman (2006) speculate, principals are frustrated, having been stripped of autonomy, which has produced "an increasingly rapid turnover of school leaders and an insufficient pool of capable, qualified, and prepared replacements" (pp. 62–63). Quinn (2002) summarizes the pressures of the modern-day principal:

> Increased job stress, school funding, balancing school management with instructional leadership, new curriculum standards,

educating an increasingly diverse student population, shouldering responsibilities that once belonged at home or in the community, and then facing possible termination if their schools don't show instant results. (p. 1)

Moreover, fewer and fewer prepared persons seek the job. According to the National Association of Secondary School Principals, half of the nation's school districts report a scarcity of administrator applicants (Quinn, 2002). The dearth of principals is particularly endemic in districts perceived to have challenging working conditions, large populations of impoverished or minority students, low per pupil expenditures, and urban settings (Forsyth & Smith, 2002; Mitgang, 2003; Pounder, Galvin, & Sheppard, 2003; Pounder, Reitzug, & Young, 2002). Evidence suggests that many high poverty districts field six or fewer applicants per principal vacancy (Roza, Celio, Harvey, & Wishon, 2003).

The fact that few aspire to the job should not be surprising. Many believe that principals must be equipped with a "suit of armor" (Sykes, 2002, p. 146). That is, there are so many demands and responsibilities placed on school principals that they must work in a reactive manner to fend off the constant bombardment of forces, both acute and chronic. The problem may be the result of the perceived impossibility of meeting the superhuman expectations of the poorly conceived image of the Great Principal as the Lone Ranger and hero.

In reality, the principal hardly acts alone. Instead, principals' actions fit into the larger school and education environment. Understanding where they sit in the education community and how their actions relate to others may take some of the pressure off fulfilling the Great Principal image. Neither full glory nor blame should fall on the principal's shoulders alone.

Decades ago, Lightfoot (1983) offered portraits of principals who do not go it alone. In one school, the principal can "track down resources and broaden horizons" (p. 42) as he builds bridges by networking with community groups and leaders to establish programs that will link students with the working world. Another of Lightfoot's principals fosters participation and collaboration. She paints him "down in the trenches inspiring, cajoling, and encouraging people to 'do their best and give their most'" (p. 68). He also serves as a buffer, protecting his faculty members so that they have the freedom to do their best. In another high school, Lightfoot (1983) illustrates how a town meeting format changes patterns of power and decision making away from the principal to the entire school community. Other examples show that an effective principal does not work alone. Louis and Miles (1990) talk about a close, cohesive internal network when describing the relationships among staff in those high schools that successfully implement change. In *Horace's School* (Sizer, 1992), teachers themselves lead the press for changes. Goodlad (1984) emphasizes the need for a skilled principal who can secure a working consensus in the search for solutions. More recently, effective principals have been highlighted by their work leading communities of practice (see Militello, Schweid, & Carey, 2008; Printy, 2008; Supovitz & Christman, 2003), taking charge of initiatives centered on the core of teaching and learning (see Elmore & Burney, 1999; Hightower, 2002), investigating policies such as student retention (see Bryk, 2003), and using data to develop new support mechanisms and to implement new teaching and learning strategies (Coburn & Talbert, 2006; Militello, Sireci, & Schweid, 2008; Supovitz, 2006). Such examples provide insights into how the school principal can debunk the myth of the great principal.

THE PRINCIPAL MATTERS

Still, the principal matters. The leadership of a principal is crucial for school effectiveness, second only to the role of the classroom teacher and the quality of the curriculum (Leithwood, Seashore Louis, Anderson, & Wahlstrom, 2005). The role of the school principal is positioned to reshape a school's culture (Deal & Peterson, 1998) and to increase achievement. However, direct causal links between leadership and student achievement have proven elusive. Nonetheless, we can connect the principal's leadership with student achievement through organizational and relational properties that create conditions and capacities to influence teaching and learning (Leithwood et al., 2005; Leithwood & Wahlstron, 2008). Specifically, different types of leadership have an impact on student achievement outcomes (Leithwood & Mascall, 2008; Marks & Printy, 2003; Robinson, Lloyd, & Rowe, 2008). Moreover, leadership has been shown to impact the creations and sustainability of professional learning communities (Printy, 2008; Wahlstrom & Seashore Louis, 2008). In short, the principal can develop school capacity. And school capacity leads to improved student achievement (see Day, Harris, Hadfield, Tolley, & Beresford, 2000; Leithwood, Jantzi, & Steinbeck, 1999; Sebring & Bryk, 2000). Research tells what the principal can do to build such capacity.

The skills, knowledge, and dispositions needed by the school principal to improve instruction have been extensively explored (Elmore, 2000, 2002b, 2003a; Hallinger & Heck, 1996; Leithwood et al., 2005; Marzano, Waters, & McNulty, 2005). Research suggests that improving student learning in schools depends on strong leadership, as evidenced by findings that school leadership through interactions with teachers accounts for one quarter to one third of the total school effect on student achievement (Hallinger & Heck, 1996). For example, a meta-analysis of empirical works conducted by the Mid-Continent Research for Education and Learning (McREL) sited the potency of specific behaviors for school leaders (see Table 1.1).

Table 1.1   McREL Behaviors Positively Associated With Changes That Ultimately Affect Student Achievement

Behavior	Definition
Flexibility	. . . adapts their leadership behavior to the needs of the current situation and is comfortable with dissent
Monitors/evaluates	. . . monitors the effectiveness of school practices and their impact on student learning
Change agent	. . . is willing to and actively challenges the status quo
Knowledge of curriculum, instruction, and assessment	. . . is knowledgeable about current curriculum, instruction, and assessment practices
Intellectual stimulation	. . . ensures that faculty and staff are aware of the most current theories and practices and makes the discussion of these a regular aspect of the school's culture
Ideals/beliefs	. . . communicates and operates from strong ideals and beliefs about schooling
Optimizer	. . . inspires and leads new and challenging innovations

These principal behaviors discovered through the McREL research are positively associated with educational leaders that can promote "second order" or systemic change that leads to improved student achievement (Marzano et al., 2005). Likewise, a meta-analysis of school leadership literature conducted by the Stanford Educational Leadership Institute found that effective principals (Davis, Darling-Hammond, LaPointe, & Meyerson, 2005) do the following:

- Develop deep understandings of how to support teachers
- Manage the curriculum to promote student learning
- Transform schools into effective organizations that build capacity for teachers to promote student learning for all students

The principal cannot simply expect teachers and other staff to engage in new actions without structures, supports, and resources. According to Newmann, King, and Young (2000), the development of a school's capacity has four core components: (1) the development of knowledge, skills, and dispositions of individuals; (2) the existence of a functional problem solving professional learning community; (3) schoolwide program coherence; and (4) availability and accessibility of technical resources to support teacher and student work. Principals are in the position to add organizational coherence, to develop a stable platform, to develop individual capacity, to develop teacher-leaders, to advocate for appropriate resources, to implement support mechanisms, and to focus the entire school community on student learning.

Perhaps James March (1978) had it right when he stated that principals are provided directions that look more like "a bus schedule with footnotes by Kierkegaard" (p. 244). Nonetheless, there are examples of principals who have acted heroically—in concert with their school, district, and school community. The journey to debunk the myth of the great principal begins with the development of a team of educators and community members that surround the child in and outside of school. Principals do not have to be the sole superhero, although they may in fact develop and lead a legion of superheroes. They do, however, need a framework or process to build teams, access their energy, and support action for improvement.

CHAPTER SUMMARY

We know schools are under fire from multiple forces. We also know how important the principal is and that the notion of the Great Principal is a myth. This chapter identified forces surrounding schools as well as specific elements that make a principal effective. Principals do not have to be superhuman, but we say they must be super principals by harnessing the forces using the power of the people in the school community to develop collaborative inquiry-action processes. In the next chapter, we describe how successful and effective school leaders do not allow themselves to be overwhelmed by the forces; rather, they harness the capacity, develop new capacity, and engage in inquiry-minded, action-oriented practice in order to leverage, buffer, and/or embrace new educational challenges. Principals of dynamic schools do this with both inquiry and action. This is not done alone. These principals lead teachers and school communities through a deliberate, mindful, focused, and grounded *collaborative inquiry-action cycle.*

Questions and Exercises for Reflection and Discussion

1. Make a table of the forces that impact schools. Across the top, list the five forces described in this chapter. You might also want to add additional forces that are unique to your school. On the side, create two rows: (1) your current educational setting and (2) a model or exemplar educational setting you want to learn more about and aspire to become (see note below). In each cell, write the challenges and the associated opportunities. *Such a table might look like the following.*

Forces

		Accountability	Diversity	Globalization	Competition	Community Relationships
Current School	Challenges					
	Associated Opportunities/ Strategies					
Exemplar School	Challenges					
	Associated Opportunities/ Strategies					

2. Create a table to demonstrate how the principal matters in your educational setting and in an exemplar setting. In each cell, write how you or the principal leads or facilitates activities in the specific categories. Then complete the row for what these practices look like in an exemplary school (see note on the next page). *Such a table might look like the following, with these possible column headings.*

How does the principal matter?

	Student Life	Student Achievement	Teacher Life	Teacher Professional Development	Parents	Other
Current School						
Exemplar School						

3. Use the completed tables to generate discussion. One strategy is to have a number of educators in the same setting complete the table. Convene the group to discuss commonalities and differences. Consider how strategies in your school can be supported, modified, or highlighted and how those discovered in exemplar schools can be adopted.

Note: The exemplar school could be a real school you know, a model school you read about, or a school you want to know about. Consider setting up an interview with the leader of the exemplary school you identify or conduct a Web-based search to obtain ways that exemplary schools have responded to challenges.

The Collaborative Inquiry-Action Cycle

Lee had accepted the superintendent's challenge and was now the principal at Marshall. Friday afternoon. The week before school opens for the year. Typical for this time of year. Teachers in to set up their rooms. Custodians still shining the floors. Problems with the bus schedule to solve. Department chairs bringing budget requests. The Parent Teacher Organization (PTO) wanting its schedule approved and posted. Some parents requesting changes in their kids' schedules. Seventh-grade English teacher announcing she is pregnant and will start leave during the semester. Lee stared at the desk and saw freshly minted office keys, gleam of new paint on the walls, name plate reading Principal, blinking light of phone messages, icon on computer screen for incoming email, constant chatter of the walkie-talkie, and piles of papers including last year's school improvement plan. First faculty meeting coming on Monday. No students yet. Lee was already exhausted.

For a while, Lee felt overwhelmed. Everyone—parents, teachers, secretaries, custodians, department chair, counselors, even the superintendent—wanted something from the principal. Expectations to bring energy to the school, to create a vision, to fix whatever problems each saw, to meet everyone's needs. Lee thought, "This feels like I was dropped into a cauldron or at least a jungle. I could drown or get lost just in the daily operations—in reacting to all that is already happening here. Technology, diversity, mandates, unions, limited resources, advocacy groups, parental concerns—the list could go on and on. I know I can manage all of this stuff—I've done it before. But I worked with others to narrow the focus onto teaching and learning."

The inquiry teams had become an essential activity at Horizon. Lee remembered, "In fact, they are what made that school so special. I didn't have to do it alone. Together we decided where we wanted to go and figured out how to get there—and tracked our progress all along the way, making changes as needed." Teams cropped up as new challenges emerged, and their work was iterative, cycling around problems of practice and action solutions. Still, the teams and their activity had not happened overnight. Lee realized that it had taken a lot of hard work, talking with teachers, encouraging, supporting, and setting goals that almost everyone shared. Lee realized that people had been willing to accept change so teaching and learning could improve. "Sure, a lot of problems still exist out there, and all the mandates and accountability demands make our job even harder, but we learned to use these external forces for our purposes instead of letting them drive us. A lot of talking about what we believed in. But what made the difference was that we took action. That is, we identified, we accepted responsibility, we planned and took action, we constantly looked back in order to move forward. We did all this in, what the literature calls, professional learning communities. As the principal, I have the power to make these communities possible. In turn, they make my job possible."

***

Lee's job *is* possible, not easy, but possible. Lee is successful because Lee works with others to be an inquiry-minded, action-oriented leader. It is all about practice! With curiosity and a sense of efficacy, this principal attends to practice and employs an inquiry-action cycle that iteratively and collaboratively frames and examines problems of practice, chooses actions to address the problems, assesses and monitors effects of these actions, and then reframes the original problems. The cycle is an ongoing system of practice. The collaborative inquiry framework combines elements of action beyond an individual school principal as activities in the cycle involve multiple participants with various areas of expertise. As new challenges, issues and problems surface, the principal includes specific resources and participants with expertise to the particular issue. Our inquiry-action principal establishes communities of practice that create changes in what people do, more than in what they say.

Most schools have written vision and mission statements that may or may not reflect what is really happening in the school and often do not serve the school as a guide for action. In many schools, the vision and mission statements are just that—statements that are not useful for practice. Because the vision is not actively lived, schools layer on programs and other strategies they believe will result in school improvement. This is the

Christmas Tree approach to school improvement—that is, adding on new *ornaments* to the school. These multiple and constant additions are reactions to external forces, perceived needs, challenges, and problems. The results are often a hodgepodge of disconnected, expensive, and often unevaluated programs, practices, and materials. Such layering inhibits coherent and systemic planning and programming and often does not lead to successful outcomes. Schools may talk about reflection and reflective practice, but such talk usually ends with a postmortem of what was not achieved. Deeper consideration and understanding of school goals and exploration of problems are often omitted when the solution is to "get a program." Addressing challenges in school improvement requires both thought and action. Our cycle couples inquiry *and* action.

This chapter introduces and explicates the collaborative inquiry-action cycle. First, we set the stage by describing collaboration in communities of practice. We also consider what it means to value action in a school.

RATIONALE FOR THE COLLABORATIVE INQUIRY-ACTION CYCLE

Principals who use a collaborative inquiry-action cycle demonstrate the antithesis of school leaders who grab for programs, layering on prescribed solutions nearly randomly with little or no evaluation. Inquiry-guided principals act but they do not rush to implement disjointed and ambiguous programs that may have worked elsewhere. Instead, they turn the spotlight on inquiry into the practices in their own schools. They recognize that schools lie within multiple and varying contexts, so as the school leader, they bring together stakeholders from the relevant contexts to engage in the cyclical inquiry process. The process leads to choices that respond to the school and its community's unique situation and needs. As a result, the school community becomes genuinely accountable for the school's work.

Because accountability entails accepting responsibility for one's actions and for reaching a desired outcome (see Newmann, King, & Rigdon, 1997; O'Day, 2002; Rallis & MacMullen, 2000), authentic accountability may begin by asking what the community considers important and what it wants its schools to accomplish. Inquiry-minded, action-oriented principals look inside the school and classrooms where instruction occurs; they question the practices, their origins, and their impact on student learning. For them, accountability means engaging in ongoing, recurring cycles of action and evaluation that provide feedback to link performance with results. Focusing on such local, professional accountability is proactive—it promotes the internal improvements that, in turn, are necessary to meet external accountability demands. Meeting national goals of improved student learning begins with local inquiry and action.

We define inquiry as a planned, purposeful, and systematic process for collecting information, decision making, and taking action as a means of contributing to improvement of policy, programming, and practice in order to increase the positive outcomes of schooling for all within the school and community (see Weiss, 1998). Inquiry is a natural human process. Think about purchasing a car or refrigerator. You went through your own inquiry cycle. You asked: What are my needs? What are my limitations? What are my options? What is known about these options? Whom do I consult? The cycle formalizes and systematizes this natural process for schools. Rallis and MacMullen (2000) outline a set of activities that make up the inquiry cycle. Based on years of research and work with schools, the specified activities in the cycle include the following:

1. Identifying the problem of practice

2. Establishing outcomes for which the school accepts responsibility

3. Articulating the theory of action

4. Identifying important questions concerning student learning

5. Taking action

6. Evaluating (conducting mindful analyses of the data in light of the desired outcomes, and interpreting information in light of the school's purposes)

7. Reflecting and start the cycle again

Use of the cycle, which begins and ends with questions of evaluation, is crucial to improving practice. The cycle repeatedly frames and examines problems of practice, chooses actions to address the problems, assesses effects of these actions, and then reframes the original problems of practice. This approach is rooted in the core assumption that student outcomes are improved through collaborative, inquiry-based processes around teaching and learning, and that leaders facilitate these processes. The inquiry-action process entails explicating what actions are taken, why, and to what effect—and then learning *from* and acting *on* that knowledge. The framework must be lived; an *inquiry-minded, action-oriented* principal believes, knows, shares, and acts the framework within the school's communities of practice.

COMMUNITIES OF PRACTICE IN PRACTICE

The collaborative, inquiry-action cycle is grounded in the belief that successful leaders for instructional improvement cannot operate in isolation. Seen as distributed rather than hierarchical, leadership is constructed of relationships rather than roles (Firestone, 1996; Halverson, 2003; Spillane, Halverson, & Diamond, 2001, 2004). Leadership involves collective deliberative decision making and "might best be defined as an interactive, dynamic process drawing members of an organization together to build a culture within which they feel secure enough to articulate and pursue what they want to become" (Rallis, 1990, p. 186). The principal's job, then, is to create such a culture of collaboration.

One structure for meaningful collaboration is the community of practice (often called a professional learning community). Such communities consist of professionals who are "engaged in the sustained pursuit of a shared enterprise" (Pallas, 2001, p. 7) and who interact with each other "in particular contexts around specific tasks" (Spillane et al., 2004, p. 5). Members of school communities of practice collaborate with the goal of supporting their work toward instructional improvement. As the name implies, communities of practice examine their own practice: They analyze data related to their work to inform their planning and decisions; the dialogue results in learning that builds coherence and capacity for change.

"Practice is the source of coherence of a community" (Wenger, 1998, p. 73), and this coherence in a school community manifests through three basic characteristics that are critical to the inquiry-action cycle: *joint enterprise, mutual engagement,* and *a shared repertoire.* Wenger (1998) defines *joint enterprise* as the meaning or understanding that the members of a community have negotiated regarding what they will mutually accomplish. We offer several steps in the inquiry-action cycle to negotiate and establish that the practice, with its attending problems, is a joint enterprise.

Mutual engagement requires that members of the community of practice interact with one another regularly to develop new skills, refine old ones, and incorporate new ways of understanding the shared enterprise (Wenger, 1998, 1999). Dialogue—that is, conversations that build on exchanges to generate new meanings—is essential to the mutuality of engagement. Dialogue is a fundamentally interactive process of authentic thinking together. It moves beyond any single individual's understanding to produce new knowledge (Senge, 1990). Each phase of the cycle relies on dialogic interchange that engages the multiple voices that constitute a school.

Finally, the community of practice develops a *shared repertoire*—that is, the "communal resources that members have developed over time, through their mutual engagement" (Wenger, 1998, p. 4). This shared repertoire may consist of artifacts, documents, language, vocabulary, routines, technology, and so on—all of which can contribute to the dialogic conversations. These anchors of coherent and purposeful interaction are normative practices for the group. The examples provided throughout this book illustrate the coherent dialogue of effective communities of practice.

CHANGING PRACTICE CHANGES BELIEFS

The product of a community of practice is action—that is, a change in practice. Changes in beliefs may accompany the change in practice initially—or they may arrive later. Far more important than what people in schools talk about is what staff members in schools *do* differently. Thus, rather than try to change what the staff thinks or believes, the collaborative inquiry-action cycle focuses on behavior. Because the human "cognitive model is not linear, . . . understanding can follow action" (Spillane, Reiser, & Reimer, 2002, p. 421). Fullan (1993) labels the sequence as "ready, fire, aim" (p. 31). He considers this alternative order fruitful for understanding organizational change: *ready* suggests direction without bogging down the process; "*fire* is action and inquiry where skills, clarity, and learning are fostered" (p. 31; italics added); *aim* crystallizes new beliefs. Simply put, belief can follow action (McLaughlin, 1990; Spillane et al., 2002). As Elmore (2002a) puts it, "Only a change in practice produces a genuine change in norms and values. Or, to put it more crudely, grab people by their practice and their hearts and minds will follow" (p. 3).

Examples shed light on the importance of actions over words. The first comes from interviews of school principals that one of us conducted during a study of inclusion in a large urban city. We asked: What "best practices" for working with students with disabilities in inclusive classrooms are emerging? What school-level strategies exist that support inclusive classrooms? The principal of a primary school responded effusively with global comments about how much she loved "the little children" and how the school was dedicated to the learning of "each and every one" through using the "best and proven teaching methods." She could not, however (even upon probing), offer examples of best practices that teachers had learned and could be expected to practice or of strategies she used to ensure that teachers used these practices in their instruction. Observed classrooms revealed traditional methods that scarcely reflected the state of the art in early childhood education. The principal uttered the language but could not demonstrate the practice.

Another example is described in the case of Mrs. Oublier (Cohen, 1990), a teacher who believes she has revolutionized her teaching of math to emphasize mathematical understanding, not mechanical memorization. Observations of her classroom, however, indicate that her instruction mixes tradition and innovation within a very old instructional framework. While her words embraced change, her practices remained much the same as always.

Finally, each of us has observed in various research studies, teachers who unofficially, but effectively, implemented a proven practice such as using data to inform their practice but who could not verbalize the rationale or articulate the outcomes. In cases of such teachers, understanding emerges from practice. All of the above examples illustrate that professionals do not always understand what they do or why they do it.

As we propose in Chapter 1, schools confront a variety of forces that demand changes. Those changes that have sustained impact are those that require school leaders, teachers, parents, students, community members, and others to behave differently. For example, talk of the benefits of mainstreaming children with disabilities did not change practice until laws were enacted that actually brought these children into general education classrooms; only then did teachers modify instructional practices. Similarly, policy discourse calling for equity and opportunity failed to eliminate tracking, whereas, the imposition of high-stakes testing has altered tracking practices in many districts. Ultimately, most teachers have come to believe that their job is to teach *all* children. Consequently, pedagogical and structural changes that manifest in actions first can drive changes in beliefs. A community of practice that is not rooted in elements of inquiry-based practice may provide only a superficial belief system without impact on practice and student achievement. A community of practice must work within a *cycle of inquiry and action*.

THE INQUIRY-ACTION CYCLE

As a regular and natural part of their ongoing operations, communities of practice in schools that embrace continuous improvement scrutinize their practices explicitly, collectively, and publicly. The school culture supports a willingness to question practice and learn from errors—a willingness to open and explore the "gap between the ideal and the actual" (Wiggins, 1996, p. 6). The process recognizes the ideal, the desired outcome, and continues with the collection and examination of data to reveal the actual.

The activities described below, taken together, constitute the collaborative inquiry-action cycle. While each activity is essential for continuous improvement, the order is not linear and may not necessarily be followed sequentially. The process is, in fact, recursive, with inquiry embedded in each activity. When practiced mindfully, the process is essentially heuristic—that is, it allows for trial and error—and encourages discovery of case-specific solutions. The antithesis of the layering process—or Christmas Tree approach—in the inquiry-action cycle encourages getting rid of what doesn't work and modifying and strengthening practices that improve student learning.

The Problem of Practice

Exactly what does the inquiry-action cycle focus on? Every school is confronted with what can be defined as problems: some that affect many, ones that touch only a few; ones that appear trivial, some that relate to processes and structures, and others important to outcomes. The cycle, however, narrows the range of possible problems to focus on issues of student learning. Without such focus, schools can be pulled in diffuse directions and accomplish little. Prioritizing and identifying those questions surrounding student learning allows the school to organize around problems of practice at the core of the school's mission: teaching and learning. The community of practice asks these questions:

- Based on experience, concerns, data, or external forces, what key questions beg our attention?
- What intriguing puzzles or troubling dilemmas related to student achievement do we face?
- Are we especially bothered—or happy—about a particular event?
- What do we do well—and how do we know this?
- What do we do poorly—and how do we know?

First, the inquiry-minded, action-oriented principal looks at where the problem comes from: Who pulled it out of the hat of potential problems? Who identified it as a question of concern? Who decides that it really is a problem? Taking a slightly different angle, what is the source of the problem? Who, or what groups, are involved? Identifying and prioritizing the problems of practice is important, but equally crucial is the recognition that each problem has an identifier and a source, which may or may not be the same person or group. In the figure that follows, we specify eight potential problem identifiers or sources. Problems or issues of concern may come from any of these sources:

- *Parents:* Why is my child not challenged appropriately? She is so talented!
- *Teachers:* We want this new brain-based curriculum, but it's not on the *What Works* list.

- *The community:* We refuse to support the two-way bilingual program anymore because it privileges the non-English speakers.
- *The school board:* Do we teach character education, and do we have a bullying policy in place?
- *The superintendent:* I have trained the teachers in differentiated instruction. Is it working?
- *State and national governments:* Why do several subgroups not make adequate yearly progress? Do your students with intellectual disabilities spend enough academic time with their nondisabled peers?
- *The principal:* Teachers should use assessment results to modify their practices so they can meet the needs of the diverse mix of students we serve.

The questions may even come from other groups, but these groups are the primary sources of questions about student learning.

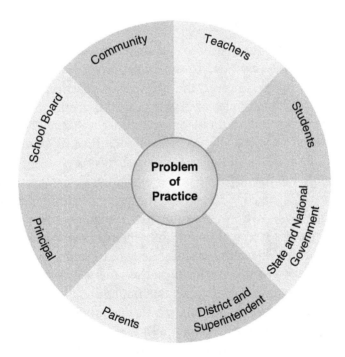

How are choices made about what to inquire and act upon? Schools that attempt to address all the problems of practice that can be identified will end up solving none, returning to a reactive, layering state. This phase of the cycle becomes explicitly collaborative as the community of practice joins in selecting problems of practice to act upon. Still, while a joint enterprise for the community, school principals play a critical role in drawing boundaries and prioritizing the identification of problems of practice.

Principals can keep the target as learning, not simply teaching or materials or structures. For example, constituents often bring specific curricular or programmatic concerns to the table without understanding the student learning perspective. The principal can ask what difference it is likely to make for student learning—both the process (how they learn) and the outcome (what they learn). Too often the problems of practices are linked to what teachers do, not to what students learn. Centering the focus on learning produces the following guiding questions to help identify and select problems or practices:

- How severe is the problem or issue for the students in our school? Does it consider all students or selected groups?
- How crucial is the problem or issue to student success, both affective and cognitive?
- How feasible is it that the school and its constituencies can make a difference in regard to the problem or issue?

The more focused the questions, the more targeted the response. That is, general questions often lead to superficial problem identification and prescriptive solutions. However, the problem of practice should not be about outcomes alone. Choice of problems is also about *who* needs *what* and *why* and about intended outcomes that are *righteous*. That is, decisions are guided by a socially just moral code that seeks to distribute resources and benefits equitably. Given the diverse student bodies in today's schools and the disparate power allocation across constituencies, educators are challenged to respond to the savvy constituents who push for benefits for a selective few. Choosing just, or equity-seeking, problems of practice captures voices of community members who may be underserved or ignored. While problems of practice can target specific groups, not all problems of practice can focus on the same selected groups.

Finally, the problem of practice should not be about only the cognitive aspects of student learning. Schools are also about developing the whole child into a critical thinker with emotional and physical well-being who participates and contributes to one's own environment. Developing the whole child means the student will be better able to make sound moral choices and contribute more fully to the democratic society and to a productive economy.

Identifying problems of practices with these principles regarding learning, equity, and developing the whole child engages the entire community, allowing all to take responsibility for their choices and move toward acceptance.

Acceptance

Once the problem has surfaced, the relevant community of practice goes to work. The purpose of the dialogue related to this phase of the inquiry-action cycle is to own the problem. That is, participants accept responsibility to take actions that lead to improvements in practice and to reflecting on that action. The dialogue begins with a set of questions:

- Does the problem really exist?
- How important is it and to whom? Who owns the problem?
- Do we agree that the problem is worth considering?
- Do we all agree on the definition of the problem?
- What do we already know about the proposed problem?
- What data or evidence do we have that this is a problem?
- Have we made previous attempts to deal with the problem?
- What do we know about these problems in other places?
- What learning expectations do we hold for our students related to this issue?
- Which students are affected by this problem—and what do they need?
- What do we expect our students to learn and our teachers to do?
- Do we accept responsibility for achieving these outcomes?

Accepting a problem of practice entails dialoguing about perceived root causes, contextual considerations, roles and responsibilities of various actors in the school community, and intended equitable outcomes (see the figure that follows). Exploring root causes requires that dialogue goes deeper than superficial or obvious explanations. For example, if third graders are not learning math, we first must discover why they are not learning math—before we jump to implementing a new curriculum or other Band-Aid solutions. Rather, we need to ask some questions:

- Are the third grade teachers qualified and able to teach third-grade math?
- Are the teachers actually teaching the curriculum?
- Are the students ready for this curriculum?
- Have we diagnosed the specific needs of each student (e.g., children may know the math but cannot read or may not know enough English)?
- Does the teacher have appropriate materials to teach the curriculum?
- Can teachers teach the curriculum using different modalities to reach a variety of students?

This list of questions goes on and on. Asking such questions uncovers root causes that give direction for potential actions.

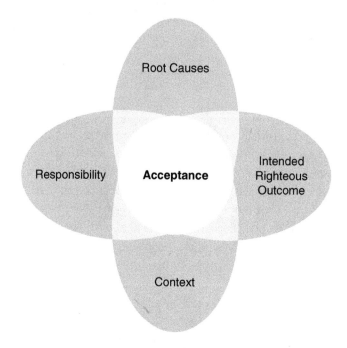

The dialogue also explores intended and fair outcomes within the local context. As discussed earlier, conversation is embedded in what is important to the community. Each school community operates with a unique set of circumstances and needs. For example, a school could map the assets that surround the school to see what is available and what is missing to meet the needs of the specific school population. Is there a specific community organization that works with children of migrant workers? Are there community health organizations willing to partner with the school? If assets exist, how will we use them? And if not, what can we do to support the identified needs? Context matters. For example, Leithwood and Riehl (2003) found that successful leaders in diverse settings focused on climate and culture building and tailored teaching and learning to their population.

Ultimately, people in the community take responsibility for change to occur. This usually begins with identifying those willing to and capable of assuming the tasks. However, principals may need to generate capacity and, at times, motivate the will of their staffs. Recognizing the root causes and moral implications of the problem and its potential outcomes as they play out within the local context, leads to accepting responsibility for the problem. This dialogue also provides direction for proposed actions.

Theory of Action

Purposeful change starts with an expression of intended outcomes and expectations: What is our goal? What are our objectives? Explicitly recognizing where we want to go is naturally followed by a consideration of why we are not yet there; thus, we revisit our problem of practice. Finally, we propose actions to get there. Such dialogue produces a theory of action, a causal or axiomatic (if, then) statement. For example, if we want first graders to read at grade level, they need decoding skills and phonemic awareness. The problem is that our general education teachers do not systematically teach these skills. In fact, some do not even have the knowledge and expertise to teach specific reading skills. This statement leads to other embedded theory-of-action statements, such as, if our students are to use decoding skills and phonemic awareness, then teachers must be trained in these areas and use appropriate strategies.

Therefore, the theory of action states both the desired outcome and the proposed actions aimed at achieving the stated outcomes. Put simply, it states what the community of practice is going to do to get where it wants to go. A theory of action is specific and focused; it presents both the means and the end. The desired outcome or the ultimate goal is agreed upon prior to the specific means to achieve these ends. Still, a theory of action is not overly simplified or general. As March and Simon (1958) warn, a "rationale theory of action calls for simplified models that capture the main features of a problem without capturing all its complexities" (p. 169). Rather, the theory of action puts forward a specific outcome goal, related to the problem of practice that is expected to result from the specific proposed action(s) necessary to reach that goal.

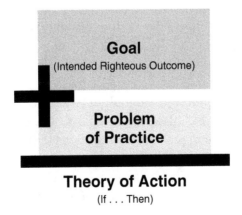

Goal
(Intended Righteous Outcome)

Problem of Practice

Theory of Action
(If . . . Then)

The simple causal statement forces dialogue around *leverage points*—that is, key components of the system around which people agree to work to realize large-scale systemic improvement. Key leverage points include resources, knowledge and skills and expertise, commitment to accountability, assessment, curriculum, capacity building, and professional development; and structure. In the example theory-of-action statement above, the leverage points are centered on building teachers' capacity to assess and teach decoding skills and phonemic awareness (e.g., professional development needs, use of diagnostic assessments). Leverage points are places to direct action.

A theory of action is the right place to start the dialogue about solutions. Rather than confining the community of practice to what they already know or what has been done in the past, a theory of action can be liberating, allowing for multiple interpretations and creative solutions. At the same time, a theory of action provides a concrete road map for taking action.

Taking Action

The next step is to move from theory of action to practice—to action! At this stage of inquiry, teachers interweave their beliefs with behaviors that, in turn, alter their beliefs. Theory of action becomes theory in use as teachers take actions they believe will lead to the intended outcomes. Then as teachers observe responses to their actions, they discover alternatives and modify actions. They ask: Are we learning how to do the best practices? Are we doing them? How are our students responding to what we are doing? Are we agents of our own practice?

Taking action is an iterative and ongoing interaction of discovery and enactment. The search process for what actions to take involves what James March (1999a) refers to as exploration and exploitation. That is, the organization and the individuals that compose it must balance the need for exploration (discovery, novelty, innovation, variation, risk taking, and experimentation) with exploitation (refinement, routinization, production, implementation, efficiency, and reliability) (March, 1999a). This open flow of ideas and the need for clear action is not easy; as March (1999b) stated, "Balance is a nice word, but a cruel concept" (p. 5). This "requires developing coupling, loose enough to allow groups to develop their own knowledge, but tight enough to be able to push the knowledge along the lines of process" (Brown & Duguid, 2000, p. 115). Nonetheless, such balance is crucial to making organizations tight enough to promote clear goals that are accountable to outcomes, with features that allow for individual participation. When a balance is struck, a window of opportunity, or local zone of enactment, may be opened (Spillane, 1999).

This exploratory search process allows actors in the organization to develop meaning and a deeper commitment to the enactment process (Rowan, 1990). Such enacting environments "gather information by trying new behaviors and seeing what happens. They experiment, test, and stimulate, and they ignore precedent, rules, and traditional expectations" (Daft & Weick, 1984, p. 288). Enactment delineates the importance of individual practice and solicits satisfaction through gratifying efforts. The discovery mode is where an organization uses carefully devised probes to get the results they originally intended (Daft & Weick, 1984). Thus, discovery and enactment lead to action.

Taking action is not void of inquiry. Teachers are, to use Donald Schon's (1983) terminology, *reflective practitioners*. They discover while enacting, and their discovery constantly informs their practice (see the figure above). This discovery process builds what is termed *teacher agency*— that is, personal creative, relevant, and situational meaning making combined with the belief that you should and can affect action and outcomes. In the taking-action phase, the inquiry-minded, action-oriented principal's role is primarily one of support for teacher agency. The role includes the following items: ensuring that teachers know what best practices are and look like and that they know how to use them in their classrooms, nurturing an environment that fosters risk taking and what David Cohen (1988) calls "adventurous teaching." The principal can allocate necessary resources to make this happen.

Evaluation

Evaluation is the "systematic assessment of the operation and/or outcomes of a program, compared to a set of explicit or implicit standards, as a means of contributing to the improvement of that program or service" (Weiss, 1998, p. 4). Intentional and utilization-focused evaluation (see Patton, 1990) requires the systematic collection of data about the processes, products, characteristics, impact, and/or outcomes of a program for the purpose of determining the merit and worth of programs, instructional activities and materials, or events. What evidence can be found to answer questions about fidelity, impact, and student outcomes:

- Is it working?
- What are we actually doing?
- What are we actually looking for?
- Is what we are doing aligned with what we intended?
- What do we want to know about what students are learning? And what is the impact on student learning and students and teacher learning?
- What else is happening to the students?

In our previous example, the training of teachers would be the first action; then, the community of practice would want to ask questions about the training: its *fidelity* (Did the training actually teach decoding and phonemic skills? And did teachers attend?) and the *impact* (Did they actually use the training in their practice? Are they using what they learned or reverting to their customary practices?). To answer these questions, the community of practice identifies and examines what was supposed to be done, looks at what was done, and then investigates the impact. For example, it may review multiple sources of evidence of the curriculum, of the training, and its delivery. For *outcomes*, the community of practice may want to look at student achievement scores. They may also want to look at artifacts of the skills put into practice. Artifacts, as we have just described, are persons, places, events, records, or materials that are manifestations or representations of learning that has occurred or changes that have been enacted (or not). The evaluation process requires judgment that is a mindful interpretation of what the artifacts mean in practice. In our example, posting of phonemic spellings may represent an artifact of the training put into use in the classroom, thus impacting practice.

The evaluation stage is another place for local democratic deliberation—necessary for pluralistic views to be expressed and heard. For evaluation to yield useful and valid information for the instructional improvement process, the dialogue spans the boundaries of the school and community; a wider school community beyond the faculty and staff joins in. Inquiry-minded, action-oriented principals encourage and facilitate a public deliberative—and respectful—dialogue that engages multiple voices that have a legitimate reason to comment on and critique school programs and instruction.

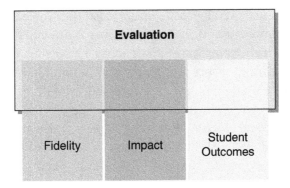

Ultimately, the community of practice accepts that the evaluation includes the essentials:

- It is an ongoing process of inquiry.
- It is essential to decision making.
- It aims to improve the lives and work of the children, teachers, and community.
- It is participatory and requires analysis and interpretation across constituency perspectives.
- It generates information to be used for improving practice.
- It is a continuous and repeating cycle.

In summary, evaluation is a tool for organizational learning and change.

Reflect and Start Again

The process does not end with an evaluative judgment. Instead, any evaluation leads to further actions. All the actors (principal, teachers, participating parents, and community members) recognize that any theory of action reflects only their best guess (albeit an informed guess) about cause and effect. Ongoing reflection is crucial to improvement: Is the evidence of the action's impact and effect acceptable, relevant, and informative? Are we satisfied with the results? If yes, what do we want to strengthen? If not, what do we want to change? Why?

Thus, reflection is more than just thinking about something: It requires experimentation, observations, and critique. The learning lies in the interaction of concrete experience, a critique of that experience, and revised actions. At its best, reflection loops back to revisit the original definition of the problem of practice, questioning its validity as a frame for action. This metareflection can lead to thinking in new ways. When the community of practice is able to reconceptualize the problem—altering the underlying assumptions and values that drove the original theory of action and, therefore, generating new approaches to solving the problem— double-loop learning occurs (see Argyris & Schon, 1974). Only when people engage in such a process can they understand the importance of knowing what to add *and* what to get rid of. The process starts over, but participants are not doing the same thing. They have learned, altered their assumptions, and changed their behaviors.

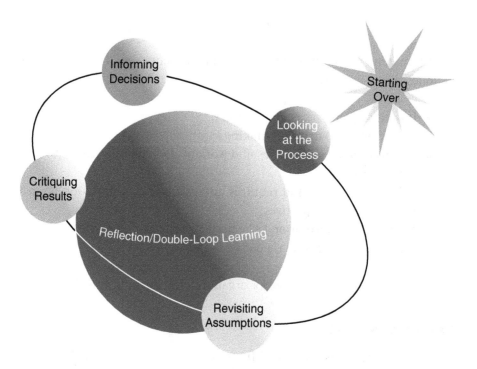

One middle-school community's solution to a long-term problem with graffiti and litter on school grounds offers an example illustrating double-loop learning. Assuming that keeping the grounds clean and graffiti free would eliminate or at least reduce incidents, the principal charged the custodial team with vigilance in maintaining the grounds. The problem continued. Next, the principal decided that if more trash barrels were placed strategically, people would be less likely to litter. No improvement. Then, he limited access to wall sections of the building during school hours and contracted a security firm to conduct surveillance after hours. He even considered requesting that a fence be built. No reduction in graffiti. "The problem is that we simply cannot prevent people from littering and painting graffiti." In fact, the severity of the problem was affecting the budget as costs for additional custodians and surveillance increased. Unwilling to give up, the principal wondered if maybe they had incorrectly identified the problem, so he called a meeting of students, parents, and school neighbors and asked them to define the problem. The ensuing dialogue revealed that indeed students were the perpetrators—they figured that, concerning litter, "that is what we have custodians for" and that "a little graffiti did not hurt anyone." A new theory of action emerged among the group: If students are charged with keeping the school clean and attractive, they will not litter or cover walls with graffiti. Everyone agreed to try morning homeroom cleanup crews and to designate the wall located by the playing fields as a graffiti wall. Almost overnight, litter disappeared and graffiti (some remarkably artistic) was contained, for the most part, to the official wall. Violations of either offense became self-policed by students.

CHAPTER SUMMARY

In this chapter, we began with a description of communities of practice. Next, we outlined an inquiry-action cycle that can be used as a framework for real change in educational settings. Adding these two elements of professional communities of practice and the inquiry-action cycle we offered the *collaborative inquiry-action cycle* (see the following figure). The activities that make up the collaborative inquiry-action cycle capture the complicated, nonlinear, iterative, and transformative interaction of behavior and thought. Engaging in the cycle creates a school that dialogues and acts and reflectively modifies its actions on a continual basis. Nothing remains static. As communities of practice that believe in organizational learning, community members accept a *culture of change* that believes that "change is the way we do things in our school, but we don't change just for the sake of changing." The change is not random or erratic; it is purposeful and planned—and constantly evaluated. Integral to organizational learning, the change is coherent, demands will, and requires building capacity. The school that lives the collaborative inquiry-action cycle balances internal professional accountability with external accountability demands.

Still, just as a principal cannot accomplish instructional improvement alone, organizational learning and improvement through the collaborative inquiry-action cycle needs a principal to bring it all together. The next chapters operationalize the cycle with contextualized examples, showing Lee working with the Marshall Middle School community of practice on curriculum, assessment, and instruction.

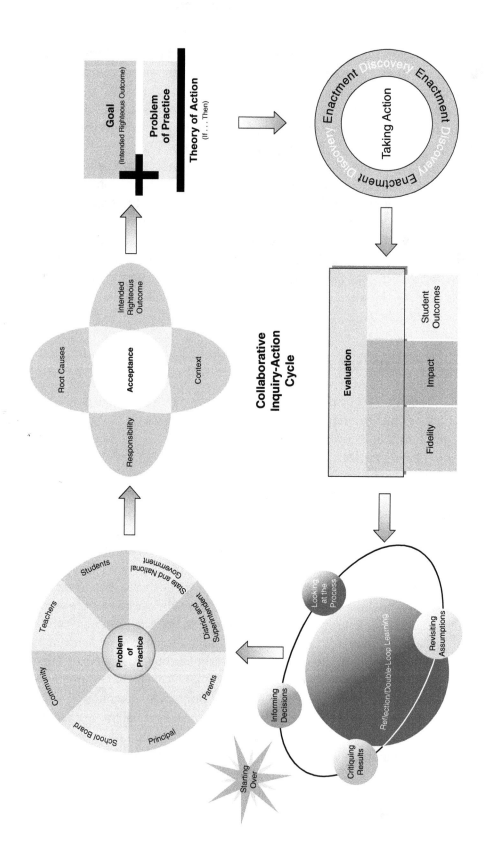

Collaborative
Inquiry-Action
Cycle

Questions and Exercises for Reflection and Discussion

1. Does your school use any part of the collaborative inquiry-action cycle?
   - If so, can you provide examples for specific steps in the cycle?
   - Who participates and what voices are missing if any?
   - What evidence do you have that any steps you may use are working?

2. If you cannot identify these steps in your school or if steps are missing, what do you see as inhibiting factors?
   - How could you use the cycle to address these factors?

PART II

The Collaborative Inquiry-Action Cycle in Action

What Are We Teaching?

A Case of Curricular Alignment

Accepting the principalship at Marshall Middle School had been the easy part. Now Lee was ready to bring people together and make things happen. Where to start? OK, any improvements in student learning had to start in the classroom. But where in the classroom? Maybe with the teachers. Or the students? What about the curriculum? The resources? The schedule? Class offerings? Student support?

The dizzying array of possibilities led Lee to construct a logical sequence of questions:

1. What are we supposed to be teaching our children at Marshall Middle School?

2. Are we teaching what we are supposed to?

3. Are we effectively teaching what we are supposed to?

4. How do we know what is effective?

5. How will we know if our efforts are working?

6. What do we do when we get answers to the above questions?

As Lee looked over the questions on the office whiteboard, certain themes emerged. Lee noticed that the first two questions focused on whether Marshall had a clearly articulated and aligned curriculum that teachers adhere to and that is monitored. Lee understood Questions 3 and 4 as recognizing teachers' needs for training and resources in order to engage in pedagogical strategies that have been "proven" effective. Question 5 raised the evaluation issue. Specifically, what are the measures of student achievement? Question 6 captured Lee's conviction that rushing to action would be disastrous without questioning what teachers were teaching, how teachers were teaching, and if students were learning. So not knowing where to begin, Lee started at the beginning—the intended and taught curriculum. That is, Lee's first task was to understand the content teachers were supposed to teach and to monitor if they were actually teaching it. Lee thought, "The faculty might resist shining the light on their practice. Still, they might be intrigued with exploring what we say we do, why, and whether we do it!"

STEP I OF THE INQUIRY-ACTION CYCLE: WHAT'S THE PROBLEM?

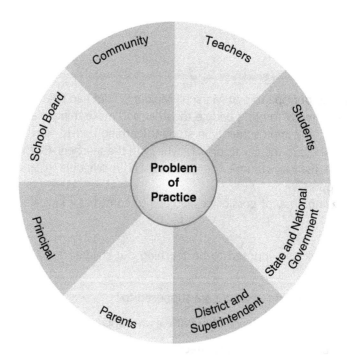

Lee understood that curriculum was an important and necessary first step in efforts to improve student learning at Marshall. After all, curriculum is the foundation of teaching. State and local education departments construct curricular benchmarks and standards to establish the content of subjects. The push for set standards and even for delineation of content contact hours (i.e., required courses) was brought to the fore in the 1960s. Two events began the formal march to standardization: Sputnik and the Civil Rights Movement. The first questioned U.S. preparedness to compete in the race for space while the other tackled issues of equality. In both cases, schools were looked on as the tonic for the exposed aliments. The mandates of this era were directed especially toward the content areas of math and science, and new requirements were imposed on America's schools. All this education reform happened quickly; by the end of the decade, integration of students and specific course requirements were fully enacted.

The 1983 report *A Nation at Risk* warned that our educational systems was "being eroded by a rising tide of mediocrity" (p. 5). On its heels, standards-based outcomes (SBO) reforms gained momentum in the 1990s. Unlike previous curricular reforms, SBO focused on achieving specific curricular benchmarks rather than completing required courses. Therefore, the content of what was being taught became the focus, and reform demanded mastery of skills and knowledge. Specifically, SBO deviated from the traditions of units, classes, and age promotion and moved toward nonlinear mastery learning. That is, the goal was that each child would master the agreed-upon standards. However, at the close of the twentieth century, SBO had become yet another term lost in the boneyard of educational jargon.

Nonetheless, curricular standards continue to drive many education reforms. Most recently, high-stakes assessment accountability calls for testing to measure student knowledge. Such assessments require an established set of content to be tested. While the current rhetoric uses assessments rather than standards, standards remain the sine qua non of useful assessments. Standards are written so that objectives can be constructed for student learning. While Plato may not have formulated specific lesson plans with corresponding Socratic objectives, certainly he gave forethought to the content of what he would address, before his oration to the gathered crowd.

Lee, having been in education for a couple of decades, has seen reforms come and go and therefore had learned well the importance of everyone working off the same baseline curriculum. Lee needed to find out if such a curriculum existed—or if the lack of one was going to be the problem. Lee also saw the ensuing discovery process as an expedient way to bring together views across community groups. Lee met with, heard

from, and read about various constituencies to learn their viewpoints on
the curriculum and standards:

- *Community:* Lee uncovered an unexpected phenomenon in regard
  to the community and their interest in curricular standards.
  Specifically, the members of the ethnic minority community organizations were most concerned with the district's work on curricular standards. For the most part, parents of successful students
  were interested only in how their children were challenged (or not)
  in regard to the curriculum. However, a number of community
  organizations offered their concerns over a standardized curriculum that was not multicultural or may lead to tracking of students
  that, they said (and Lee discovered the data supported) has been
  historically disproportionate to minority students in remedial and
  special education courses. Members of these organizations were
  not against standards but asked, "Whose standards are these and
  are they inclusive of people like us?"
- *State and national government:* As Lee discovered, federalism is alive and
  thriving in the United States. The founders forged a government that
  ensured states' rights. While educational reforms have often sought
  national-level reforms, states have held firm their right to interpret and
  enact reforms at the local level. The 2002 reauthorization of the
  Elementary and Secondary Education Act (ESEA), No Child Left Behind
  (NCLB) was a recent effort to make national-level reforms. To a great
  extent, it has succeeded. There was an initial call to develop a national
  curriculum and to use the National Assessment of Educational
  Progress (NAEP) as a national measure of student learning. However,
  states have resisted this, and NCLB has allowed each state to develop its
  own curricular standards and their measures. In Marshall's state,
  English, math, and science standards have been established and benchmarks for each have been set from grade to grade.
- *School board:* The school board in Marshall's district has pushed the
  district administration in three areas: (1) adherence to the state
  curricular benchmarks, (2) the creation of a curricular framework
  in social studies even while the state struggled to create a set of
  social studies standards, and (3) the development of a set of remedial and advanced courses in Grades 6 through 12.
- *District and superintendent:* In response to the school board, the district has created a set of documents called "Pacing Guides." These
  documents highlight the specific state-level standards that are to be
  taught by grade level and by content at each grade level. The district
  also established a social studies curriculum subcommittee that has

been struggling with a set of standards for more than three years. Finally, Fran, Marshall's superintendent, called for an increase in Advanced Placement courses in the district's high schools, increased enrollment in seventh-grade algebra, and remedial courses in English and math in Grades 7 through 10.

- *Principals:* District principals were expected to implement the district responses. However, Lee recalled principals' viewing the changes as superficial. For example, while principals handed out the Pacing Guides, the guides were not used as part of the principal's evaluation of teachers. Additionally, the creation of new remedial courses and the increased enrollment in advanced courses led to inequalities in the student demographics of classes. Principals were unable to monitor multiple curriculums in their own schools.

- *Parents:* The two sets of parents who were most often heard were those seeking assistance for their struggling students and those seeking academic rigor or placement in advanced courses for their children. In the past, Lee rarely had complaints of a teacher not teaching the curriculum; more common were complaints of teaching style. However, as standards are being tested, more and more parents are becoming savvy of *what* teachers are teaching, in addition to *how* they are teaching.

- *Teachers:* Teachers contended that while the time allocated to assessments has increased, the breadth of intended curriculum has simultaneously expanded. That is, with every addition of a curricular benchmark or standard, the reciprocal deletion of benchmarks or standards has not occurred. Teachers complained of the sheer number of standards listed in the district's Pacing Guides. Additionally, teachers of art and physical education are troubled by the recent scheduling of students out of their classes and into remedial math and English. The "double-blocking" of math and English has left students without "exploratory" courses. Lee was also struck by the number of teachers who had requested teaching assignments at a grade level that was not tested by the state. In one case, a seventh-grade math teacher was upset by the uproar as his students' poor performance on the state math assessment was published in the local paper. Finally, a representative for the teachers' union warned that a grievance would be filed if a teacher's academic freedom were to be violated by mandates concerning what and when things were to be taught.

- *Students:* Students began to exhibit frustration regarding the limitations in the choice of courses they could take. Specifically, many students were no longer able to take some of their favorite courses, such as art or physical education. Some students also described how homogeneous their classes were becoming. They complained that they were moving from class to class with the same group of students.

Lee came to understand that the curriculum was indeed a "problem of practice" at Marshall Middle School.

Lee's review of the district's current curricular Pacing Guides in math and English for Grades 6–8 at Marshall exemplified the issue—too much to be covered and too little time. Working with the Marshall community of practice, Lee asked the teachers to review these guides related to their own practice:

- Do you teach this? If not, why not?
- When do you teach this?
- What do you teach that is not on the Pacing Guides?

Table 3.1 is an excerpt from the Marshall Middle School Eighth-Grade Math Pacing Guide, and Table 3.2 is the accompanying rubric the school's math teacher completed.

This process was helpful. Just a glance at one pacing guide was enough for Lee to realize that teachers were being asked to cover too much. Lee thought that the sheer magnitude and vast scope of the standards would yield coverage that would be a *mile wide and an inch deep*. The completed rubrics and subsequent analyses did reveal that not all teachers were teaching to all the skills; many teachers had *pet projects* or taught to other skills that were not linked to the standards, and no patterns appeared in the delivery of the content.

In the end, the team identified a number of assessment problems of practice:

1. Teachers are asked to teach and students expected to master too many skills each nine-week period.

2. The breadth of the curriculum does not allow for time or space for remediation, advanced learning, or mastery.

3. No one monitors teachers' adherence to the Pacing Guides.

4. Many teachers continue to teach skills and projects they "liked" or "have always done" regardless of the skills and standards in any given nine-week period.

5. Teachers are not provided time to sequence their curriculum within grade, to map skills among grades, or to dialogue about specific skills and/or projects certain teachers are interested in or effective at teaching.

Table 3.1   Marshall Middle School Eighth-Grade Math Pacing Guide

<table>
<tr><td></td><td>**Unit and State Standards**</td><td>**Math Skills to Be Taught and Assessed**</td><td>**Vocabulary**</td><td>**Process Skills**</td></tr>
<tr>
<td rowspan="3">**First Nine Weeks**</td>
<td>Basic operations with variables</td>
<td>Number sense and numeration that will be taught and assessed

1. Evaluate expressions containing variables and exponents

2. Evaluate real numbers and algebraic expressions using correct order of operations</td>
<td>Sum, difference, product, order of operation, whole numbers, fractions, addition, subtraction, multiplication, division, quotient, variable, algebraic expression, power, exponent, base, grouping symbols, equation, solution, inequality, real number, stacked bar graph, number line, origin, graph, visual model, ordering, opposite, velocity, absolute value, matrix, commutative property of addition and multiplication, associative property of addition and multiplication, additive and multiplicative identity, coefficient, like terms, reciprocal, rate, ratio, similarity linear equation</td>
<td>Communication

• Communicate math thinking clearly to teachers and peers

Reasoning

• Recognize and develop math arguments and proofs</td>
</tr>
<tr>
<td>Basic operations with real numbers</td>
<td>Numeric and algebraic operations and analytical thinking

1. Solve equations and inequalities using mental math

2. Develop algebraic models given real-world situations</td>
<td></td>
<td>Connections

• Able to connect math concepts in other contexts

Representations

• Select, apply, and translate among math representations to solve problems</td>
</tr>
<tr>
<td>Linear equations</td>
<td>Data analysis and statistics

1. Interpret tables and graphs

2. Construct and interpret appropriate tables and graphs given various data</td>
<td></td>
<td>Problem solving

• Solve math problem in other contexts</td>
</tr>
</table>

Table 3.2   Pacing Guide Rubric

	Math Skills to Be Taught and Assessed	Do You Teach These Skills? If Not, Why Not?	When Do You Teach These Skills?	List the Skills You Teach Not on List and Rationale	Describe Any Major Projects With Associated Skills
Number Sense and Numeration	• Evaluate expressions containing variables and exponents • Evaluate real numbers and algebraic expressions using correct order of operations				
Numeric and Algebraic Operations and Analytical Thinking	• Solve equations and inequalities using mental math • Develop algebraic models given real-world situations				
Data Analysis and Statistics	• Interpret tables and graphs • Construct and interpret appropriate tables and graphs given various data				

Lee feared that this set of problems was leading to misguided teaching practices, at best, or had become a barrier to student learning, at worst. Lee repeated this exercise with the school's English teachers.

In the end, Lee and the teachers revealed the problem of practice as, *The Marshall Middle School math and English intended curriculum did not match the actual taught curriculum.* Getting the faculty to accept that this problem of practice was real at Marshall Middle School would be the next important step.

STEP II OF THE INQUIRY-ACTION CYCLE: ACCEPTANCE

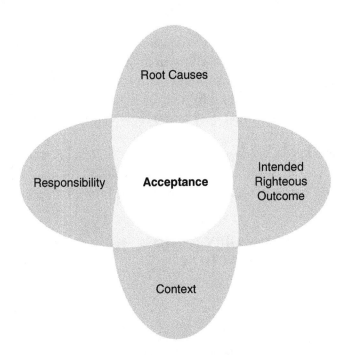

Gaining acceptance for the problem of practices is not easy. The rubric exercise provided a great number of insights into what was actually being taught at Marshall Middle School. The next activity in acceptance would involve teachers' investigation of root causes, contextualized, and intended righteous outcomes and responsibility. Lee presented the data analyses to the middle school math and English language arts (ELA) teachers. Lee did not have to do much talking—the data told the story. At first, teachers became defensive. Even though data reports did not name individuals, a number of teachers quickly provided rationale for why they had not covered certain skills. Lee allowed this to go on for some time, then moved to divert the conversation by putting up more slides. These revealed the problems beyond the one topic of not teaching to the current Pacing Guides. Now the conversation became a meta-analysis of the actual skills themselves, of the link to the state-approved benchmarks that the state assessment measures, to the inefficiencies associated with teachers covering the same standards among grade levels, and subsequent results that certain students were never taught all the standards.

This data-based dialogue provided a window into what was really happening in classrooms at Marshall. The dialogue also allowed for the development of a consensus of the intended righteous outcomes in math and ELA for all students. Lee began to hear teachers talking in axioms:

- "If we can collaboratively reconstruct the Pacing Guides, then we have ownership and we will want to follow them."
- "If I gave my highly successful math fractions project to the sixth-grade teachers and taught them how to include this in their curriculum, then I would not have to reteach fractions the next year."

Soon teacher talk seemed to move toward the next stage of the cycle, the construction of a formal theory of action. This was all the confirmation Lee needed that the teachers had truly accepted the problem of practice.

STEP III OF THE INQUIRY-ACTION CYCLE: THEORY OF ACTION

A theory of action is specific and focused. That is, the desired outcome or the ultimate goal is agreed upon prior to deciding on the means to achieve such ends. Additionally, a theory of action is not overly simplified or general. Rather, the theory of action posits a precise outcome goal. Such explicitness allows for the coupling of leverage points and activities in an effort to achieve the outcomes. In this step of the collaborative inquiry-action cycle, the theory of action and leverage points are articulated.

Lee and the math and ELA teachers revisited the problem-of-practice statement and created a goal statement: *To improve learning for all students in English language arts and math.* The theory of action emerges from the outcome and the specific problem of practice:

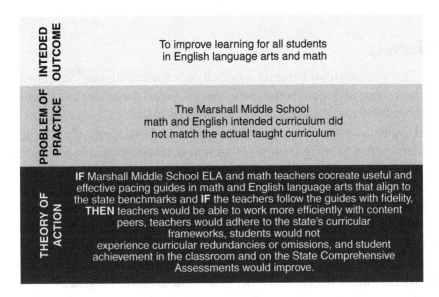

INTEDED OUTCOME	To improve learning for all students in English language arts and math
PROBLEM OF PRACTICE	The Marshall Middle School math and English intended curriculum did not match the actual taught curriculum
THEORY OF ACTION	**IF** Marshall Middle School ELA and math teachers cocreate useful and effective pacing guides in math and English language arts that align to the state benchmarks and **IF** the teachers follow the guides with fidelity, **THEN** teachers would be able to work more efficiently with content peers, teachers would adhere to the state's curricular frameworks, students would not experience curricular redundancies or omissions, and student achievement in the classroom and on the State Comprehensive Assessments would improve.

Formalizing the axiom captures both the input and the output and thus provides a new direction in the dialogue. Now teachers were interested in getting started. Much work lay ahead, but what it would take was becoming clear. And everyone would be working together. Such solution-driven and collaborative work can generate enthusiasm—and results show in both teachers' practice and student outcomes.

STEP IV OF THE INQUIRY-ACTION CYCLE: TAKING ACTION

The work to create a new set of Pacing Guides began with revisiting the rubrics teachers completed previously. The process of discovery began with expanding the rubrics to get every skill, project, and interest on paper. This discovery process would also include making the breadth of unattainable standards manageable. Subsequently, the math and ELA teachers would enact the new Pacing Guides. That is, the standards and skills would be put into play every day in every classroom.

Discovery

The teachers used hanging sheets of paper with "stickies" to show the current scope and sequence of their classes. Colored markers were used to highlight skill and standard omissions and redundancies. This activity created dialogue about both teaching content and pedagogy. For example, teachers began to horse-trade projects; that is, teachers came to realize that some of their teaching was misaligned with the standards and willingly gave up special-interest projects if teachers at other grade levels were willing and able to take them on. Oftentimes, the development of one's capacity to take on another project was led by the other teacher, who would become a mentor and content expert. This discovery was organic and iterative. However, it also revealed a problem that had yet to be addressed: How do teachers make the current *supersized* curriculums manageable?

Lee had anticipated this dilemma. Conducting scope and sequence sessions without modifying the skills and standards would be like a dog chasing its tail. Lee introduced a way to delineate standards. Familiar with work on "power standards" (see Ainsworth, 2003; Reeves, 2002) and Grant Wiggins and Jay McTighe's (2005) work called *Understanding by Design,* Lee worked with the math and ELA teachers to engage in a similar process:

1. Identifying important or essential understandings

2. Linking local curriculum to the state standards and benchmarks

3. Distinguishing among standards for enduring qualities and leverage points

4. Developing a new set of local standards based on this work

Enactment

The math and ELA teachers completed the new Pacing Guides and then redesigned the format and redrafted the language so that the guides were user-friendly. In fact, the guides were written in "kid-friendly" language. As a result, the guides did not simply sit on shelves, ignored and gathering dust. Lee was pleased to see them open on teachers' desks and to hear them at the center of content team discussions. Lee also noticed teachers' increased confidence as they presented material and discussed assignments with students—confidence that Lee attributed to a sense of agency due to their deeper understanding of what was expected and of what they were responsible for. The guides were also shared with parents, who began to refer to them when asking questions about their children's progress. Lee overheard one parent's comment to a math teacher: "Wanda was all over the house last night measuring things for a chart. I went to that guide you sent home to see why. Gosh, it makes sense, so I joined in— I could ask her questions and talk with her about what she was doing."

Enacting the new guides also led teachers to further discovery. They began to use the guides in innovative ways. For example, a new plan was afoot—a committee of teachers had emerged, seeking to create an alternative report card that used language straight from the Pacing Guides. As the teachers became invested in teaching the specific skills, they were better able to communicate with the parents and students regarding achievement levels on specific skills.

STEP V OF THE INQUIRY-ACTION CYCLE: EVALUATION

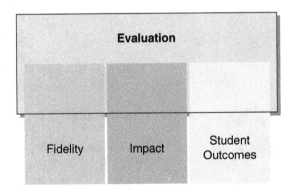

Because the Marshall teachers were instrumental in the creation of the new Pacing Guides, they knew what the content was and wanted to follow it. Thus, their use was true to the intent, and fidelity was not an issue. Additionally, Lee began to monitor adherence to the guides during instructional walks and in formal observations. In discussions and in observations, Lee felt that the new Pacing Guides were having an impact on teaching and learning. Lee also found that parents were appreciative of knowing more about the content their students were learning. One mother told Lee that it became easier for her to work with her child when the standards were not written in "education" language. The mother said, "I do not know what 'nontraditional genres of literature' means. However, I do know that the poet Maya Angelou is not a White male!"

But how did Lee know for sure that the goals were being enacted and that students were learning the curriculum objectives? What data indicated improvements in student learning? A number of teachers provided anecdotal evidence of student-learning gains. Additionally, the teachers and Lee were keeping a close eye on the State Comprehensive Assessment (SCA) scores. However, they would need years of data on the SCA scores to pass judgment on the results. One ELA teacher asked Lee if they had access to an assessment that could measure the specific skills they were teaching within each grade level. Because teaching had become more focused, she wanted to know if there were better ways to assess student performance on what she actually was teaching. One clear impact, then, was that teachers were witnessing the connection between curriculum, instruction, and assessment.

STEP VI OF THE INQUIRY-ACTION CYCLE: REFLECTION

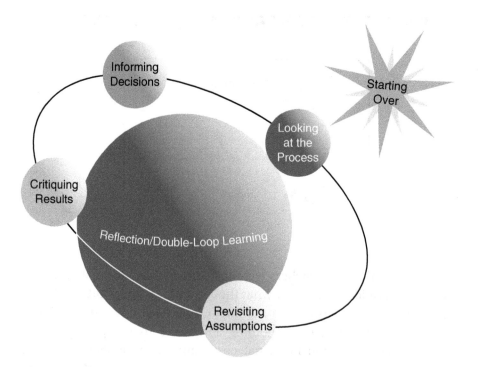

Evaluation activities inspired reflection—which requires more than mere thinking; reflection requires critical analysis. Such reflections are not easy. Critiquing one's own work can be uncomfortable at best; critiquing work among colleagues can feel dangerous. Barriers have to be removed and safety zones established. Perhaps one of the most important lessons

Marshall's teachers learned was about their own potential to innovate and implement real change in schools. They could collaborate with purpose, and they could fix something, such as the curriculum, that was broken. And if they had done it once, they could do it again. Lee noticed a huge change in the way teachers approached their work—and each other. Even the way they walked down the hall and greeted others was improved—now people smiled and talked. The establishment of the collaborative inquiry-action cycle enabled teachers to engage as professionals who define their work and enact it to serve their students' learning, as well as to prepare them to meet external demands and standards.

So with increased degrees of confidence and comfort, the faculty began to think beyond what they had accomplished: We have a curriculum; we are using it; we like the results of having and using a curriculum. What next? As Lee knew well, reflection cannot end with thinking and analysis. By definition, reflection leads to consideration of future actions that might modify or alter current practices. Lee encouraged Marshall's faculty to explore what questions had arisen out of their articulating the curriculum and developing Pacing Guides. What might be missing? What new problems might have emerged now that we are doing things differently? Thus, having completed the cycle, Marshall's faculty restarted at the beginning.

CHAPTER SUMMARY

With Lee's guidance, Marshall Middle School had established that they wanted to improve student learning in English language arts and math. They had identified and accepted the problem that the school's math and English teachers were not teaching to an understood and shared curriculum. Recognizing a goal and a problem of practice led to stating a theory of action: **IF** *Marshall Middle School ELA and math teachers cocreated useful and effective state Pacing Guides in math and English language arts aligned to the state benchmarks, and if the teachers demonstrated fidelity to the guides,* **THEN** *teachers would be able to work more efficiently with content peers, teachers would adhere to the state's curricular frameworks, students would not find curricular redundancies or omissions, and student achievement in the classroom and on the State Comprehensive Assessments would improve.*

Next, the math and ELA teachers and Lee produced these guides. Then, they proceeded to use the guides in multiple venues: for classroom instruction, for communicating across the community, for initiating changing practices beyond the classroom. Evaluation indicated that teachers were using the guides with fidelity with positive impact on their sense of professionalism, on students and parents, and on their relations with each other.

However, satisfied with curriculum and Pacing Guides in place, Lee and the faculty knew that the change work was not done. Together they entered a new inquiry-action cycle. In the next chapter, we follow them dealing with challenges related to assessment and using data to improve instructional practices.

Questions and Exercises for Reflection and Discussion

1. Consider your school's curricular scope and sequence:

   - When was the process done? Recently?
   - Who among the current teachers participated? Who did not?
   - Was the process conducted with content specific teachers across grade levels?
   - How relevant is the scope and sequence to the current standards in your state?

2. Consider your school's Pacing Guides:

   - Which content areas are covered? Which are not? Why?
   - Who among the current teachers participated? Who did not?
   - Was the process conducted with content-specific teachers across grade levels?
   - How relevant are your Pacing Guides to the scope and sequence?

3. Consider your school's Pacing Guide rubrics at the classroom level:

   - Have rubrics been developed for each classroom? If not, why?
   - How relevant are the rubrics to the current Pacing Guides?
   - How are the rubrics used? What evidence do you have of their use?
   - In what ways do school administrators monitor the use of these rubrics?

4. Use the collaborative inquiry-action cycle to create, review, or modify your school's curriculum.

   - What are your **problems of practice**? How do you know this is a problem? What stakeholder groups do you have and need information from?
   - What will your plan of action look like for **acceptance**?
   - What might a **theory of action** look like in your school?
   - What is your plan of action for **taking action**? What information did you **discover**? What is the plan for *enacting* the action?
   - How will you **evaluate** what you do? What are your tools and metrics for *fidelity, impact,* and *outcomes*?
   - How will you ensure that the process you undertake is **reflected** upon? In what ways might the curriculum change as a result of this process?

What Do We Know?

A Case of Data Informing Practice

Lee's superintendent was crystal clear—turn Marshall around. Of course, Lee understood that this explicitly meant: "Improve the state standardized test scores at Marshall Middle School!" And Fran had said: "Don't forget DDDM." Sure, Lee knew the acronym for data-driven decision making and wanted to make informed decisions that would focus on teaching and learning. Lee laughed, "Aren't all decisions data driven?" Still, questions arose: What data were available at Marshall, how were the data used, and were teachers capable of using the data to improve their teaching?

Here is what Lee did know:

- The state office of accountability wanted state standardized test scores to improve from year-to-year and they wanted to know how schools were measuring progress in between annual testing.
- The school board wanted district schools to continue to administer a national, norm-referenced assessment each year to compare local scores with other schools across the nation.
- The superintendent and the district's new assessment director wanted to invest in a districtwide assessment system that would measure individual student growth from year to year.
- The district's principals wanted to invest in a districtwide assessment system that would evaluate students at "benchmarks" within each year.

In the midst of these pressures, Marshall's department chairs came to Lee to report low morale among teachers as a result of the publication of state assessment results in the local newspaper. To make matters worse, recent reports said that teacher merit pay may soon use the state assessment results as the metric for bonuses. Additionally, Lee's first meeting with the Parent/Guardian-Teacher Organization at Marshall uncovered two factions regarding state scores. One group was concerned that there was too much emphasis on the state test scores, while another group worried that teachers were not teaching closely enough to the state-mandated curricula. The minutes from last year's student government meetings were especially troubling to Lee. In the April meeting, students were bothered by the amount of time they spent taking assessments. One student reported feeling anxious to the point of not wanting to come to school.

Lee knew that data in many forms were key to improvement. Lee also knew that not having enough data or the right kind of data would only exacerbate the problem. A "problem of practice" was emerging. There was some good news—Lee's previous collaborative work with the staff on curricular alignment would allow the school's staff to focus on *how* to measure learning, not *what* should be measured. Lee understood that the staff at Marshall would have to engage in another iteration of the *collaborative inquiry-action cycle* to find a solution.

STEP I OF THE INQUIRY-ACTION CYCLE: WHAT'S THE PROBLEM?

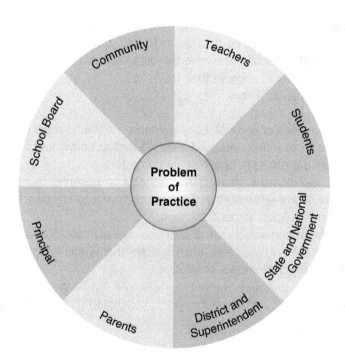

Concern about assessing students is not new to schooling. From early IQ testing to simple classroom testing to standardized state and national testing, assessments have exhibited different forms and functions. Currently, high-stakes accountability uses state-level test scores to determine student, teacher, and school success. This emphasis on standardized scores has placed assessment in the political spotlight and in the minds of every school educator.

Traditionally, assessments have been the weak leg in the tripod of curriculum, instruction, and assessment at the school level. Moreover, the identification of "assessments" as a problem of practice cannot be considered in isolation. The issue of assessment needs to be interpreted in the local context, embedded in curriculum, and must inform instruction.

Consequently, to understand and fully identify the problem of practice, Lee recognized the perspectives of the various constituency groups that needed to be heard and considered:

- *Community:* Generally speaking, community members pay attention to property values. An important variable to property value has been local schools. Rankings of local schools have focused on standardized test scores, chiefly college entrance assessments such as the ACT and SAT. However, since the Adequate Yearly Progress (AYP) stipulations of the No Child Left Behind (NCLB) legislation, individual schools are "graded." These scores are publicized in the local media as well as real estate publications. Since many businesses and families who live in the Marshall catchment care about property values, they also care about the test scores.

- *State and national government:* NCLB of 2002 required that all states administer a state-level common assessment. These assessments are used to determine AYP for local schools. While the function of these assessments is clear, the form of the assessments varies from state to state. Like most states, the one in which Marshall is located refined an existing state assessment aligned to the state-approved curriculum. To some extent, Marshall is lucky because it is not in one of the states that uses national assessment instruments such as the SAT and ACT that are based on national curricular standards. The state is considering joining the more than 10 states that have been granted permission to use "student growth" assessments that calculate student growth from year to year. In all cases, these assessments are a summative measure that is given at the end of the year. Recently, the state's education department accountability office asked schools and districts to identify additional assessments that are used to monitor achievement between annual state assessments. Finally, Marshall faces federal "requests" to administer the National Assessment of Educational Progress (NAEP).

- *School board:* The school board in Marshall's district wants a national test to compare their local students with their national peers. A number of such assessments that normalize scores among grade-level peer groups exist for such a purpose (e.g., Terra Nova, Stanford, Iowa). The Marshall Board adopted one of these assessments last year.

- *District and superintendent:* In response to these governmental and school board pressures, the district's superintendent, Fran, is considering purchasing or developing additional assessments to be administered between the state assessments. However, what these assessments are to measure has been contentious. Some personnel want an assessment system that measures student growth from year to year. Other personnel want an assessment that has the ability to predict passing or failing rates on the state-level assessment.

- *Principals:* The district's school principals are worried about adding assessments. Specifically, they are concerned over the administration of the assessments and the uses of the assessments. While at a meeting with principal colleagues, Lee heard principals' concerns regarding asking teachers to administer and students to take yet another test. They were also worried about the person power it would take from the school's administration and counseling offices.

- *Parents:* Parents have a clear goal; they want their children to do well. The most visible measure of "doing well" is classroom grades and standardized test scores. Therefore, they want good grades and high scores for their children. Parents also want to be sure that their children are taught what will be tested. This is especially true in Marshall's state since it has high-stakes accountability. That is, in order to graduate, students must pass the state's comprehensive exam. Consequently, many parents exercise their knowledge (accurate or not) of Marshall's teachers to position their students in specific classrooms. Where once, many Marshall parents chose teachers according to personal and pedagogical styles, many parents today are becoming informed and influential consumers of the curriculum.

- *Teachers:* "Teaching to the test" has become a negative mantra of many Marshall teachers. They contend that this type of teaching is de-professionalizing their practice, making the profession programmatic and limiting the improvisation and relationship-building many see as critical to learning. Finally, teachers recognize that relevant assessment results can be used to improve teaching.

However, the current battery of assessments is not designed to provide such relevant, useful data for teachers, further confusing their efforts and stealing from the time needed to improve achievement results for each child.

- *Students:* Anxiety and assessment are not unique to middle school students. However, as the stakes of assessments at Marshall have increased (e.g., determining grade promotion, graduation, or merit scholarships), student anxiety has increased. As a result, students have a vested, but unacknowledged, interest in the types, results, and uses of assessments. Students view schooling as a learning process. While assessments are integral aspects of learning, when students become inundated with assessments and when students are not always provided detailed information concerning the assessment results, they become detached. Consequently, assessments and learning are not often associated together by students.

All of these pressures put Lee in an all-too-common and complex position; no principal can adequately address all the concerns of all these constituencies. However, as an *inquiry-minded, action-oriented principal,* Lee uses these complementary and competing viewpoints to carefully construct a problem of practice. Clearly, school-level assessments are a problem. For Lee and Marshall Middle School, the problem of practice is to articulate and implement a coherent and aligned assessment protocol. In an attempt to refine the problem of practice, Lee decides to use Marshall's "community of practice," specifically the School Improvement Team (SIT), to identify the scope and sequence of assessments at Marshall Middle School.

The team began with creating a school "data inventory." Components of the inventory included all of the following elements:

- *Data and target population:* What type of assessment, evaluation, survey, and so forth is administered?
- *When and how administered:* When are the data collected? Are the data in an electronic format?
- *Type of data received and feedback:* Are the data summative or formative? Norm referenced or criterion referenced? Who analyzes the data and when is feedback provided and to whom?
- *Readiness:* What are the resources (i.e., professional development activities) and support mechanisms (i.e., time to discuss the results) associated with the data?

Table 4.1 is the completed Marshall Middle School Data Inventory for Math and English Language Arts (ELA).

Table 4.1   Marshall Middle School Data Inventory

Data and Target Population	When and How Administered	Type of Data and Feedback	Readiness
State comprehensive English language arts assessment (Grades 6–8)	Spring, electronic	Criterion (state curricular benchmarks), item-level results; results in fall	Trained to administer test and to read results
State comprehensive math assessment (Grades 6–8)	Spring, electronic	Criterion (state curricular benchmarks), item-level results; results in fall	Trained to administer test and to read results
Gates MacGinitie reading (selected sixth graders)	Fall and spring, scan sheets— electronic	By student; results within two weeks	Literacy specialist discusses results with teachers
Stanford math (eighth graders)	Fall, computer	Norm referenced by math strand; results in spring	None
Math textbook end of unit tests (seventh graders)	Every six weeks, paper and pencil	Criterion (district curriculum); teacher discretion	None
Climate survey (Grades 6–8)	Spring, scan sheets— electronic	Student perception; late spring	None
Writing prompt (eighth graders)	Four times/year, paper rubrics	Criterion (district curriculum); teacher discretion	Eighth-grade teachers provided time to discuss results and to create reteaching activities
District math assessment (Grades 6–8)	Four times/year, paper and pencil	Criterion (district curricula); Two-week feedback window	Administrators trained to facilitate conversations about curricular adherence

Missing from the data inventory was more information about *fit*, which Lee thought of as (1) what the assessment was designed for, (2) the intended uses by the end users, and (3) how the assessment was actually used. Lee often thought that in the press to make data-driven decisions, many educators were using data inappropriately. Lee jotted down all of the assessments and which constituent group's needs were being met (see Table 4.2).

Table 4.2   Marshall Middle School Data "Fit"

Data and Target Population	Fit		Constituency Group
	Purpose	**Marshall Use**	**Group**
State comprehensive English language arts assessment (Grades 6–8)	State to determine adequate yearly progress (AYP)	None	National and state government
State comprehensive math assessment (Grades 6–8)	State to determine AYP	Student remedial placement	National and state government
Gates MacGinitie reading (selected sixth graders)	To evaluate school reading grant	Limited use by reading specialist	External grant funder
Stanford math (eighth graders)	District-level officials to compare achievement with peers across the country	None	School board
Math textbook end-of-unit tests (seventh graders)	Summative evaluation of student achievement	Summative evaluation of student achievement	Seventh-grade teachers
Climate survey (Grades 6–8)	Evaluation of school climate	School improvement planning	School leadership
Writing prompt (eighth graders)	Formative evaluation of student achievement	Formative evaluation of student achievement	Eighth-grade teachers
District math assessment (Grades 6–8)	Evaluation of student achievement	None	District-level administrators

Lee's initial hunch was on target. To begin, some of the data were used in ways that were not intended. For example, teachers at Marshall were using the State Comprehensive Assessment (SCA) to place students in remedial classes by curricular strands in mathematics. However, the SCA does not provide enough data by specific curricular strand to make such judgments. Next, Lee noticed that the constituency groups that were conspicuously missing from the data inventory were teachers, students, and parents. More specifically, lacking was a set of assessment data that teachers use in a real-time, daily basis to inform their practice.

Lee brought the table to the team to examine the scope and sequence of assessments at Marshall Middle School. The team discovered that a large amount of time was spent preparing for or administering assessments each year. Next, the types of assessments were discussed. The team found that most of the assessments were summative in nature. Specifically, a number of the assessments provided data to teachers, but the timing or type of data did not allow for follow-up activities. The team's analysis also revealed the lack of perceptional data from both teachers and students. Specifically, while the annual climate survey provided important data, the team wanted to know more about how teachers felt about teaching math and ELA, and how students perceived their learning of math and ELA.

In the end, the team identified a number of assessment problems of practice:

1. Too many assessments were administered.

2. The purpose of many assessments did not *fit* the actual uses of the data.

3. Assessments did not provide perceptional data from teachers and students in math and ELA.

4. Data feedback reports were not timely and not always in a digital or electronic format.

5. Teachers lacked time and capacity to use the data appropriately.

The problem seemed clear to Lee: the teachers at Marshall Middle School do not have student-level diagnostic data needed to inform their daily pedagogical decision making. However, given the various perspectives of the multiple constituencies, Lee knew that to move forward, at least the Marshall community of practice would have to accept a shared definition of and responsibility for the problem.

STEP II OF THE INQUIRY-ACTION CYCLE: ACCEPTANCE

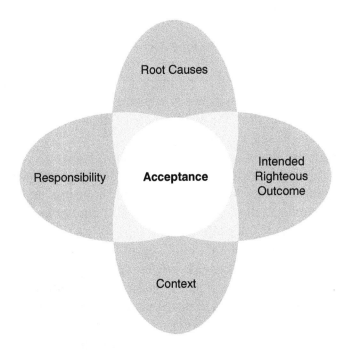

Because so many different constituents have stakes in specific types of assessment data, owning this new problem of practice may prove especially difficult. First everyone needs to agree a problem exists. The Marshall data inventory tells a compelling story that highlights the lack of student math and ELA diagnostic data. Moreover, previous efforts to address this gap led to thoughtful efforts that were not systemically implemented. Additionally, as local or individual efforts were created (e.g., eighth-grade writing prompt by eighth-grade ELA teachers and seventh-grade math unit tests by seventh-grade math teachers), no simultaneous efforts were made to remove other assessments to relieve the problem of overtesting students.

Gaining acceptance of a new assessment to provide student-level diagnostic data throughout math and English subjects at Marshall would require understanding the root causes, stating the contextualized outcomes, and, ultimately, assuming responsibility for those outcomes. For Lee, this process would begin with building consensus around the root causes. For this problem of practice, the root causes became evident: (1) New assessments were being added in response to constituency concerns; (2) when assessments were added, others were not removed; and (3) no assessment provided teachers, students, and parents with student-level, curriculum-aligned, electronic, real-time data. As a result, acceptance began with acknowledging what developments had taken place over time that put Marshall in the predicament of not having useful data to inform instructional practice.

Lee could see that the SCA math and English data revealed deficits in individuals' learning, as well as inequities across groups. Because righteous outcomes are important for this principal, Lee believed that local data could be even more powerful in getting teachers to accept the problem. Specifically, directly seeing evidence of injustice could shift their will (motivation) to accept the problem and to increase their capacity (skills and knowledge) to address the problem.

Lee began the acceptance process by establishing a subcommittee of the school improvement team called the Marshall Data Group. As this group reviewed the data inventory, important, inclusive, and deliberate dialogue occurred. Over time, consensus was built that ultimately fostered acceptance among the full staff.

Getting to this point of the collaborative inquiry-action cycle is not easy. In this case, Lee had to guide teachers through a process whereby they would accept responsibility to address the identified problem. Teachers came to understand and accept that the problem of practice would not only require the addition of a student-level diagnostic assessment system, but the use of such a system would impact their practice.

STEP III OF THE INQUIRY-ACTION CYCLE: THEORY OF ACTION

Goal
(Intended Righteous Outcome)

Problem of Practice

Theory of Action
(If . . . Then)

The ultimate goal for Marshall Middle School was to improve student learning. As written, the goal is too general. Because of the federal and state mandates and sanctions, as well as district and community pressure associated with the State Comprehensive Assessment, the Marshall Middle School goal became: *To improve student scores in English language arts and math on the State Comprehensive Assessment.* To target the SCA, Marshall needed to be sure that the intended curriculum was aligned to what was assessed on the SCAs, teachers were teaching the intended curriculum, teachers had the necessary content knowledge and pedagogical content knowledge, and teachers had multiple forms of data at their disposal that would assist them in making daily decisions about their practice. The last supposition is the focus of this problem of practice. Specifically, *teachers do not have student-level diagnostic data needed to inform their daily pedagogical decision making*. The theory of action emerges from the outcome and the specific problem of practice, which in this case is as follows:

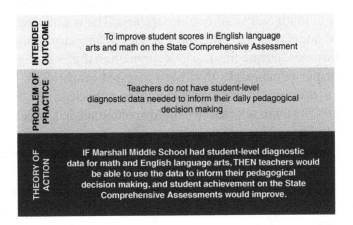

Articulating the theory of action enables new strategic dialogue. Specifically, the strategies of what is needed and what activities must take place are focused on the vision of achieving the theory of action. Strategies include specific leverage points. Such leverage points form what needs to be done to support and resource the pending actions.

STEP IV OF THE INQUIRY-ACTION CYCLE: TAKING ACTION

Taking action begins with a process of discovery. In this case, discovery included the development of a student-level diagnostic assessment at Marshall Middle School. Enactment means putting the assessment information to use. Specifically, how the tool is actualized. We begin with the process of discovery at Marshall Middle School: How did Marshall select a new assessment? What resources and supports were put in place?

Discovery

The Marshall Middle School Data Team had a task to identify an assessment instrument that would provide detailed, student-level diagnostic data in math and English language arts. The team knew that they would need a tool that was criterion referenced. Specifically, they needed a tool that would measure the district's curriculum that was aligned to the state curricular benchmarks that were assessed on the SCA. The team identified a number of products that were publicized as "formative" assessments. The team selected two highly recommended, widely adopted assessment companies to present to the team.

During the presentations, it became clear that each assessment system had strong features in regard to psychometric properties, data-warehousing abilities, and reporting features. Lee continually reminded the team to think about the issue of assessment fit and the accepted problem of practice.

The first assessment product provided student-growth data in reading and math. This product was a computer-based, adaptive assessment. Students would each have different questions based on how they answered the previous question. The advantages to such an assessment were as follows:

- The product provided excellent student reading and math data longitudinally. That is, one could chart growth in reading and math from year to year.
- The product provided curricular recommendations based on the assessment results.
- The product promoted its ability to prognosticate student results on the SCA.

The team had specific misgivings about the product:

- Because the assessment was an adaptive, computer-based assessment, teachers were concerned about the inability to help administer the assessment to special needs students.

- This assessment product did not provide teachers with results by item level. In fact, teachers would never see the actual questions!

The team determined that while this assessment product would be useful for district administrators to track individual student growth, it did not meet the specific needs revealed in Marshall's problem of practice. That is, this assessment product did not fit their needs.

The second product was also a computer-based assessment. This product allowed local educators to determine which curricular strands would be tested. Additionally, the system would assess students on forthcoming curricular benchmarks. The team determined the following advantages of this assessment:

- Teachers would receive assessment data of specific curricular benchmarks of their choosing.
- Teachers could use the results in their quarterly reporting of student progress.
- Teachers would receive data on what students already knew about future units.

Disadvantages included all of the following information:

- The curricular benchmarks that were assessed were not specific to their state. Rather, because this assessment company worked in a number of states, the curricular benchmarks were not specific from state to state.
- The team discovered that the assessment asked as few as one question per curricular strand. It concerned many team members that the reports may state deficiency in an area based on only one question.
- While the team found assessing benchmarks yet to be taught advantageous, they also feared that such a small number of items would not help them ascertain mastery. Moreover, team members were concerned that students would develop anxiety over items that they had not received instruction on.

This process of discovery revealed that there were many assessment products, all were expensive ($8–$12 per student), and each had its own definition of "formative." What the team became sure of was that neither product "fit" the needs identified in their problem of practice.

Based on the discovery process, the teachers and Lee agreed to develop an assessment that would be *informative* rather than *summative* or *formative*.

Specifically, it was decided that an assessment needed to "fit" the teachers' need to have real-time, student-level diagnostic data in math and ELA. Additionally, the assessment needed to have value for students and their parents. The assessment needed to have utility and importance to students and parents so that students could better understand their learning and parents could have a vehicle to ascertain the children's needs. What the teachers discovered was that the action they would enact would be the development of their own *informative* assessment system: the Marshall Assessment of Progress (MAP).

Enactment

Lee drew from Marshall's site budget to contract with testing experts at the local university to work with the Marshall math and ELA teachers in developing a psychometrically sound assessment. This work included the development of questions, the creation of question distracters, and a process called item-response theory (IRT) to determine acceptable scaling of questions from grade to grade. Additionally, the teachers made sure that the questions that were being developed were in alignment with the curriculum to be taught each quarter.

The MAP was designed to assess ELA and math skills and knowledge on a quarterly basis in Grades 6–8. Beyond subject content questions, each assessment would ask students and teachers a set of perceptional questions. For example, if multiplication of fractions is being taught in Grade 6, students would be asked how they learn this task best and teachers would be asked to respond to their content knowledge and pedagogical skills in regard to this topic.

The "real" enactment would come with the administration of the ELA and math MAPs and the subsequent evaluation.

STEP V OF THE INQUIRY-ACTION CYCLE: EVALUATION

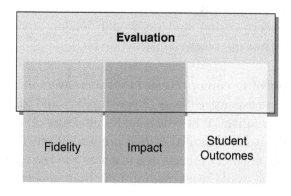

How did the MAPs work at Marshall Middle School? Lee knew that the discovery and enactment processes were important to the development of the MAPs, but Lee realized that the utility of the MAPs would be marked by three important characteristics or measures: (1) fidelity, (2) impact, and (3) student outcomes.

Lee felt confident that the math and ELA teachers were faithful to the MAP process. In fact, the department chairs worked closely with both the teachers and the technology support personnel to make sure the assessments were administered on schedule and that the electronic results were reported back to teachers within 24 hours of the assessment. However, teachers reported a lack of fidelity among students and parents. That is, students and parents were not using the MAP data. Consequently, Lee and the teachers needed to understand why. Was the MAP data inaccessible? Was it accessible, but unintelligible? Was it accessible and intelligible, but lacking mechanisms to trigger action? And what would that action look like, and were parents and students prepared to take such action? One strategy to improve fidelity included a decision that all teachers would use the MAP as a grade in their grade books. While there was some original resistance by some teachers, they soon found redundancy with their own end of marking period assessments. As the MAP became more refined, the fidelity by teachers and students also became more refined.

In regard to impact, Lee asked parents to complete a short survey during parent/guardian-teacher conferences about the MAPs. While parents were generally in support of the MAPs, many reported difficulty using the results at home. This information would influence what the teachers at Marshall did with the MAP data in the future, as will be discussed in the next section. Teachers also contributed to evaluating MAP impact. Lee held a number of meetings with the math and ELA teachers that were devoted to the MAPs. The groups discussed the impact of the assessments on their teaching. Overwhelmingly, the teachers reported finding the data useful. Still, many reported that they simply did not understand exactly what to *do* with the data. This discovery led to reflections regarding what results should trigger instruction. Such reflections are examined in the next section.

The most critical of evaluation questions is rooted in the question of student learning. Specifically, were the students advancing their knowledge and skill on the MAPs? Because the MAPs were in the initial stages of implementation, the teachers understood that this year's data would provide a baseline to be used in the future. However, teachers did report antidotal and grade book data that reflected improvements in student learning. Lee had also suggested that future research should link the MAPs to the SCA. Lee agreed to ask the university to help develop such a study.

STEP VI OF THE INQUIRY-ACTION CYCLE: REFLECTION

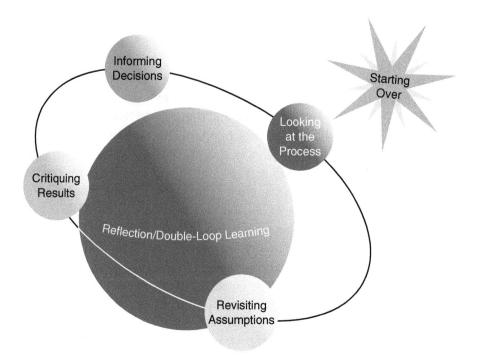

Having evaluated fidelity, impact, and outcomes of the MAPs, teachers at Marshall Middle School could engage in reflection. This process of reflecting on the MAPs allowed the teachers to think and dialogue about what they had learned and what next steps they might take. They considered the following: (1) what they were (and were not) doing with the MAPs results, (2) glitches in the MAPs questions and administration, (3) impact on the students and parents, and (4) support and resources needed to more effectively and thoughtfully use the MAPs.

To begin, the teachers wanted to provide resources that would allow parents to support student learning based on the MAPs results. Specifically, while the MAPs gave parents a lot of detailed information on their children's learning, teachers wanted to create a set of resources for parents that were aligned with the specific skills and knowledge students needed assistance in. For example, the teachers discussed developing online tutorials for each of the standard strands. These tutorials could be sent home with the MAPs results.

Discussion turned to aligning the school's quarterly report cards with the MAPs. Teachers found that the data reported on the MAPs provided greater detail than the generalities reported on marking cards. One teacher sketched out a report that would provide the home with more information (see Table 4.3).

Table 4.3   Data Analysis Exercise

State Standard (strand)	Specific Skill	Teacher Assessments (including MAPs results)				Resources
Multiplication of fractions	In this quarter, the students should be able to multiply simple fractions such as 1/3, 1/4, 2/3, 3/4					Link to on-line tutorial and/or resources to help students learn this skill

Teachers also reflected on the need to develop trigger mechanisms. Specifically, the teachers wanted the MAPs results to trigger certain actions for different groups of students based on the results. For example, teachers suggested reserving two days each quarter after the results of the MAPs to (1) meet with fellow grade-level teachers and content experts to discuss pedagogical options for students who did not meet the standards and (2) to reserve time to engage in specific strategies such as short term grouping for reteaching.

Reflection revealed additional resources teachers needed to better serve their students. For example, the perceptional data collected that asked students how they learned the specific content best also asked teachers to access their own comfort level and confidence in teaching the specific standards. As a result, teachers were forthright with their short-comings and wanted resources to address specific identified needs.

Finally, the reflections surfaced concerns about the amount of testing that occurred at Marshall Middle School. While the school had added a missing data set to their data inventory, other assessments were not removed. Lee discussed which assessment(s) teachers wanted removed. Interestingly, rather than list a set of assessments administered by the district, the teachers began with a set of assessments they used in the classroom. Specifically, as previously discussed, the ELA and math teachers discovered that the MAPs were a credible assessment of student learning and should be incorporated into the grading process. Nonetheless, Lee intended to ask district administrators to relieve them of the requirement to administer a nationally normative assessment each year.

Such reflections among Marshall Middle School faculty suggest some double-loop learning. The inquiry-action process truly became a cycle that identified new problems of practice that needed to be addressed, thus ending at the start of a new inquiry-action cycle.

CHAPTER SUMMARY

While the business community has used the evolution of data, information, and knowledge to develop strategic plans, schools and data continue to have a disjointed relationship. The U.S. Department of Education's (2003) document titled *Using Data to Influence Classroom Decisions* states, "Research shows that teachers who use student test performance to guide and improve teaching are more effective than teachers who do not use such information" (p. 2). Nonetheless, educators (both teachers and principals) are provided with little training in the use of data and feel disengaged from the planning process of collection and inspection of achievement data (Earl & Katz, 2002; O'Day, 2002). This has created a number of consequences, intended or not, including teaching toward the test and, in the worst cases, cheating on the state assessments.

Studies have illustrated that under norms of collaboration, data can be used in a nonthreatening and effective manner (Wayman & Stringfield, 2006; Young, 2006). Where assessments focused on instruction, student diagnostics, and teacher professional development, educators developed efficacy toward assessments (Stecher, 2002). The implementation of a formative assessment system must be accompanied with the development of a data-driven professional learning community. Only then can assessments move away from summative measures *of learning* to informative metrics *for learning* (see Popham, 2008; Reeves, 2004; Stiggins, 2005). In this case at Marshall Middle School, these assertions held true. At Marshall, the collaborative inquiry-action cycle enabled educators to engage in a process of transforming data into knowledge that informed their teaching. In the end, the process led them to take the following actions:

- Articulate and cull standards that align with the state curricular framework
- Develop a school level data team
- Create a district and school assessment inventory
- Develop a psychometrically sound and aligned informative assessment that provided student-level diagnostic data
- Designate legitimate time for educators to work within and across grade levels and content areas

- Gain access to pedagogical and content area professional development and coaches
- Develop rituals of use and trigger mechanisms that are frequently monitored and supported

In the end, the State Comprehensive Assessment and the host of other formative and summative assessments proved insufficient to provide Marshall's teachers with data needed to change their practice. In the next chapter we examine the challenges associated with using data to change instructional practices.

Questions and Exercises for Reflection and Discussion

1. Does your school have a data inventory? If not, use the sample inventory Lee used (or create your own) to collect the information needed to complete the inventory. What does the inventory tell you about data in your school? What data are missing?

2. Describe the "fit" between the data your school has and the intended uses. Consider using the school data "fit" table Lee used (or create your own) to understand the data "fit" issues in your school.

3. In what ways are your assessments directly connected to the scope and sequence, Pacing Guides, and corresponding rubrics? If they are not, use your reflection work from Chapter 3 to create a new or revised assessment plan (see below).

4. Use the collaborative action-inquiry-action cycle to create, review, or modify your schools assessment plan.
    - What are your **problems of practice**? How do you know these are problems? What stakeholder groups do you have and need information from?
    - What will your plan of action look like for **acceptance**?
    - What might a **theory of action** look like in your school?
    - What is your plan of action for **taking action**? What information did you *discover*? What is the plan for *enacting* the action?
    - How will you **evaluate** what you do? What are your tools and metrics for *fidelity*, *impact*, and *outcomes*?
    - How will you ensure that the process you undertake is **reflected** upon? In what ways might the assessment system change as a result of this process?

What Do We Do in the Classroom?

A Case of Changing Instructional Practice

Lee's head ached and eyes blurred. Too much staring at the State Comprehensive Assessment (SCA) scores. "At least," Lee thought, "the school is looking at scores differently." Having grown to respect what data could tell them—and finally having relevant data—teachers had asked Lee to be specific about where the school's weaknesses on the test lay. The patterns were clear—the English language learners (ELL) were failing. For Marshall's Grade 8 ELL students, an astounding 72 percent failed mathematics and 79 percent failed science. Across all middle school grades, Lee saw that former ELL students, those officially considered to have reached English proficiency, 51 percent failed math and 53 percent failed science. This subgroup was certainly not making adequate yearly progress (AYP); their failure rates were two to three times greater than for other students.

There were more scores to confirm the pattern. Across all three grades (sixth, seventh, and eighth) Marshall's teachers were administering formative assessments in English language arts (ELA) and math that were aligned with state benchmarks and the district curriculum. These real-time tests provided information for teachers and were supposed to be used to diagnose learning problems at the individual student level. Lee was not sure teachers were using these test results yet to inform their teaching, but the scores did confirm that certain students were not meeting specific curricular benchmarks—neither in ELA nor in math. Among those who were failing were many ELL students. So the problem appeared to be real—and extended beyond math and science.

Lee wondered, "What am I supposed to do? We've trained our ELL teachers to meet the state curriculum benchmarks. Our curriculum is aligned with these standards—and our tests measure what is in our curriculum. We're keeping ELL classes relatively small. We move kids out of the language development programs when they are ready—not too soon, but before they begin to lose motivation. What more can I do? Just tossing more resources to the ELL programs and teachers cannot be the answer, even if I had the resources. I need to know where to target the efforts. But where do I begin?"

To make matters worse, another pattern had emerged beyond the SCA scores. Special education referrals were skyrocketing in all grades. Teachers in core subjects of ELA and math were complaining that fewer and fewer kids were mastering the material. They were demanding a multitude of various interventions—some wanted one special program, while others wanted another. Nearly every day, another teacher's request for some professional development opportunity showed up on Lee's desk. As with the ELL, Lee knew that a shotgun of resources would not change things. Lee felt overwhelmed—and tired.

Lee yawned and stretched. "Why am I asking what I should do? I know what I need to do—NOT do it alone. This is not my problem alone—it is the school's problem, so I need to get us working together on how we are going to deal with it. Anyway, I don't even really know what the problem is. Sure, our ELL kids are failing, and lots of kids seem to be developing a special need. We need to get to the root of the problem: Who are these kids who are failing—who are not able to do the assigned class work? What else is happening in their lives (after all, they are in middle school)? What are their specific learning problems—is it one problem or many? Are teachers prepared to meet their needs? Do teachers even know what their needs are? Is our curriculum offering what we need to offer—or does it ignore certain kids or groups of kids?"

Ironically, while more questions buzzed around in Lee's mind, the principal felt hopeful. Recognizing the issues of ELL failures and overreferral to special education as a starting point for reflective inquiry that could lead to action made solutions seems attainable. "First, we have to define the problem of practice—and finally we have data and people to work with the data so we can define it with focus. Of course, folks will have to accept the problem as ours, but again, explaining the problem through our data will help. Then together we can move to action plans. We've done this before. Together we have reformed our curriculum and created a new assessment system. So I'll bring together an inquiry group. I will include teachers who can see the patterns and who are affected, along with some parents. I am also going to reach out to the owners of businesses that hire recent immigrants in the area. That's where I'll start."

STEP I OF THE INQUIRY-ACTION CYCLE: WHAT'S THE PROBLEM?

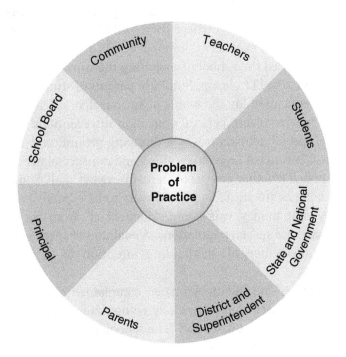

While the concern seemed specific to two subgroups of students, ELL and children with special needs, nearly everyone in the school and beyond felt the effect. Thus, identifying the problem of practice would require input from a range of school community stakeholders. The inquiry group Lee constructed would serve this purpose. On the surface the problem seemed straightforward: ELL students were not mastering academic skills and too many children overall were being referred for special services. However, the group quickly saw that different interests in the school community took different views of the problem:

- *State and national government:* The state labeled schools that did not make AYP as failing schools. As a result, the superintendent was upset that the ELL subgroup's scores would put Marshall into that failing category. From the district central office perspective, the problem lay in the classroom with the ELL teachers.
- *School board:* The school board was concerned with the increasing referral rate because providing special services costs money. The board asked if the problem was due to an increase in disability or

to the inability of teachers to meet needs of students in general classrooms.

- *Parents:* Parents of ELL students were angry because they felt that insufficient resources were directed to programs that would raise their children to levels where they could learn and compete with native English speakers. Some demanded bilingual programs; others accused the school of assigning the worst or least-qualified teachers to the ELL classes. Similarly, parents of students referred to special education lay the blame at various doors: Teachers did not know how to teach, general education interventions were inadequate, special education was a dumping ground and was underfunded. Parents of English-speaking and nonspecial needs students questioned whether any problem really existed at all. Some believed that failures among ELL children were to be expected; many were angry that money was being "sidetracked" from their children to serve these special populations. A coalition of "Citizens for Gifted Education" emerged, demanding attention to their children's needs.

- *Community:* The business owner complained that his workers lacked necessary skills, especially computation and English communication. He put it simply: "The schools are not doing their jobs in preparing future workers."

- *Teachers:* General education teachers complained that students simply could not do the work. They blamed learning disabilities, emotional problems, and parents' lack of involvement with their children's learning. ELL teachers dropped the problem into one of three categories: excessive demands on them and insufficient professional development, inappropriate materials and programs, or lack of support from families at home.

- *Students:* Students who were struggling with learning, whatever the reason, were frustrated and often acted out. Nearly all students sensed teachers' frustrations.

Lee doubted if any of these views fully recognized or accurately identified the problem. Lee told the group: "Reminds me of the Sufi parable of the man who finds his neighbor looking for his lost key under a street lamp, not because that was where he dropped it, but because that was where the light shined. Each of us is looking only where we can see."

Because Marshall now had data in many forms, Lee reminded them, they could shine the light over more area and look more closely at what was actually happening with student learning. Suggesting that the group first establish "the facts," Lee initiated the process. The following information was uncovered from existing data and other documents:

- On the SCA, ELL students across all grades did not show mastery in math and science.
- The Marshall Assessment of Progress (MAP) assessments used by general education classroom teachers revealed that students who had been in ELL less than a year ago were failing in the reading component of the ELA test and math and that many general education students were also struggling in these areas.
- Marshall math and science curriculum for Grades 7 and 8 required substantial content area reading.
- The MAPs also revealed that many general education students in Grades 7 and 8 also had difficulty in reading. Specifically, the MAPs highlighted certain ELA skills that were problematic: comprehension, sequencing, processing.
- Grades 7 and 8 had extremely high referral rates (18%) to special education. Many of the referred students had formerly been ELL students.
- Teacher-assistance team records indicated that referrals were primarily related to reading problems or for behavioral issues.
- When tested, the students with behavioral issues also showed difficulty with reading.

The group's inquiry pointed to poor reading skills as the source of the problem. Lee knew, however, that to stop at defining reading in general as the problem of practice would not be enough to build an effective plan of action. "Just providing remedial reading is not a fix; it's more of a Band-Aid. We need to determine the root causes. Why can't our kids read?" The group could say that *Marshall Middle School students are having trouble in core subjects and possibly with behavior because they have not mastered reading skills.* The group could also judge this to be a problem of practice worthy of attention because it affects student learning, it seeks equitable and righteous outcomes for students, and it concerns more emotional aspects, as well as cognitive.

Now Marshall teachers needed to accept the problem as theirs and assume responsibility for improving student reading. Thus, Lee encouraged the group to explore further, to shine the light into the classrooms and on instructional practice. To do so, this group realized its limitations—all teachers needed to be on board. This group decided to present the information so everyone could share and accept the problem of practice.

STEP II OF THE INQUIRY-ACTION CYCLE: ACCEPTANCE

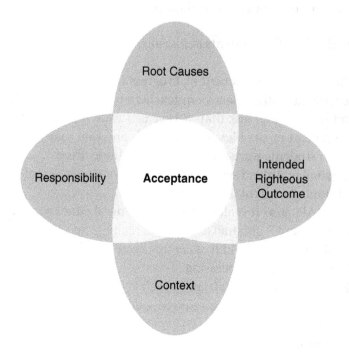

Marshall Middle School teachers were willing to explore the problem of practice that *students are having trouble in core subjects and possibly with behavior because they have not mastered reading skills*, because it displayed itself daily in their classrooms. Everyone agreed that the problem was real. Many openly admitted that they had given up trying to meet their students' needs in reading—and had been referring students for help outside their classrooms. In essence, they had relinquished responsibility. Lee knew that to deal with the problem, teachers needed to reassume responsibility, to own the problem. Lee asked for volunteers for class visitations: Teachers could volunteer their class for a visit from the principal or a colleague; the visitor would observe and script the activity and as much teacher-student dialogue as possible. At least a dozen teachers volunteered, and at least as many classes were observed. Volunteers brought their data to the next faculty meeting, where Lee facilitated a discussion of what they had seen.

Observations supported the point that many students could not read at expected levels. Thus, referrals to special education were high and ELL students' achievement was poor due to the same root cause: low literacy and reading readiness levels. But the faculty asked: Why? Most of the faculty was not surprised that observers had seen little differentiated assistance during instruction. Individual needs were not diagnosed and addressed. Help came in the form of repetition or more practice—drill and kill. Teachers followed the materials unvaryingly, pushing ahead to cover the material, even when some students clearly did not understand. While teachers administered the MAPs regularly, they seldom used the results to modify instruction, to teach from an alternative perspective, to allow some students more time, or to create short-term regrouping strategies. Students who struggled with a concept or assignment, continued to struggle as the class moved on.

Despite a district curriculum that was aligned with state benchmarks, a surprising number of teachers still "did their own thing." For example, one teacher who observed a seventh-grade science class reported, "[The teacher] had all this stuff on minerals. I asked him why. He said, 'Yeah, I did this when I was in college, and I liked it. The guy down the hall does gems. He likes them.'" Others reported similar experiences, and teachers admitted that whenever they felt they could escape from what one called "the standards straightjacket" they went off into their own interests.

The conversation turned to explanations and rationalizations:

- The pressure and demands for covering the material (How can we take time to assess and modify when we have to cover what will be tested?)
- Inadequate, insufficient professional development (I just really do not know how to teach comprehension/sequencing/and so forth, if the kid does not know it already.)
- Ineffective professional development (I went to that session on reading in the content area. Some "guru" rambled on for an hour and then put us in groups to use his protocol. What a waste!)
- Too many priorities (Everything seems important—I cannot just teach anymore. I cannot do it all, so I just do a little bit of everything.)
- Programs and interventions as Band-Aids (We have so many programs for so many different needs—I just give up and make a referral to special ed, so they can figure out what will work.)

Soon the tone became personal and local; the community demographics had changed, and individual teachers did not feel prepared:

- We have a challenging situation here at Marshall Middle; we still have families who have lived here forever—and we have a lot of new immigrants. I really want to see the new kids catch up, but I never learned these instructional strategies Lee talks about. I mean, what does it *look like* to differentiate? What does Lee mean when we are told that our challenge is to "manage heterogeneity"?
- I thought we had more kids with disabilities, but now I see that many never learned basic reading and communicating in English.

I guess that affects all their studies—and their behavior. I'd be bored and act out too if I could not take part in the class because I did not know what was going on. It does not seem fair to punish kids for something that is not their fault.

- Still, I see some kids get bored for the opposite reason. Marshall has some really talented students—in all our programs—who do read well already. Some kids who get it really quickly. We have to be sure we don't ignore them.

Lee summarized the apparent acceptance of the faculty with these words:

We, here at Marshall, take responsibility for helping ALL our students to learn to the best of each student's ability. By the time they leave us after the eighth grade, we expect students to be able to decode, comprehend, sequence, process, problem solve, and apply these skills to materials in all core subjects. This means that some will meet our standards quickly and move on, while others will need additional specific help. We won't be satisfied with inequitable allocation of resources and attention. We will have to diagnose needs, differentiate instruction, monitor progress, and check alignment. We must agree that our curriculum and corresponding instruction match our goals for our students. To do all this, we may need professional development to build teachers' capacity to provide the appropriate instruction.

STEP III OF THE INQUIRY-ACTION CYCLE: THEORY OF ACTION

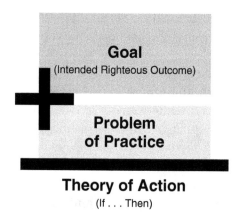

Goal
(Intended Righteous Outcome)

Problem of Practice

Theory of Action
(If . . . Then)

As before, the Marshall Middle School faculty agreed on the goal to improve student learning in ELA, math, and science, in order to reduce referrals to special education. They now realized that to do so, they needed to improve students' reading skills. The desired outcome was that all students could read with comprehension in the content areas, and thus take agency for their learning in the various subjects without the individual education plans (IEPs) of special education. Thus, the amended goal became to improve reading skills and comprehension. The problem of practice the faculty identified and accepted was that students brought a diverse set of skills and learning needs and that current instructional practice was not able to meet the multiple needs. While data were available through the MAPs, teachers often did not know how to use these data to diagnose and then design or modify their instructional practices. Teachers needed ongoing and supported professional development that was embedded in their subject matter and their classroom activities.

Put simply, both ELL and general education teachers realized that were they to use instructional strategies chosen to fit the individual reading needs of their students, the children would master the skills required to progress in the various subjects. The result would be increased achievement and fewer referrals to special education. Rather than further categorize students for remedial interventions or focus their efforts on structural mechanisms to reduce referrals (both of which too often lead to short-term solutions), the inquiry turned to teacher learning and improved instructional practice. Rather than spend resources on remediation of specific groups, resources would be directed to build all teachers' capacity to teach reading, both directly as skill development and indirectly as reading for comprehension in content areas, as needed. These proactive changes in instruction would generate changes in student performance, with an ultimate positive outcome on scores as well as referrals.

Linking the goal with the problem yields the "theory of action":

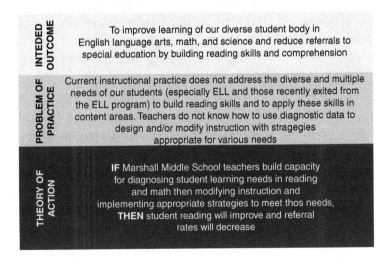

INTEDED OUTCOME	To improve learning of our diverse student body in English language arts, math, and science and reduce referrals to special education by building reading skills and comprehension
PROBLEM OF PRACTICE	Current instructional practice does not address the diverse and multiple needs of our students (especially ELL and those recently exited from the ELL program) to build reading skills and to apply these skills in content areas. Teachers do not know how to use diagnostic data to design and/or modify instruction with strageies appropriate for various needs
THEORY OF ACTION	**IF** Marshall Middle School teachers build capacity for diagnosing student learning needs in reading and math then modifying instruction and implementing appropriate strategies to meet thos needs, **THEN** student reading will improve and referral rates will decrease

STEP IV OF THE INQUIRY-ACTION CYCLE: TAKING ACTION

With a clearly articulated theory of action in place, the school community is ready to put the theory to use. Taking action means enacting the IF of the theory of action statement—in this case, building teachers' capacity to diagnose student learning needs in reading so that they can—and do—modify instruction and implement appropriate strategies (best practices) to meet those needs. The process begins with intensive and effective professional development, in using both the diagnostic tools and specific best practices in reading instruction. Lee knows that the mere availability of training does not guarantee improved instruction and is keenly aware that much of what is sold as professional development is ineffective—a lot of one-shot in-service sessions only tangentially related to core academics. Thus, Lee facilitates mini-inquiry-action cycles among grade-level groups to specify teachers' needs and identify the best way to meet those needs. Through these minicycles, the teachers recognize their need to refine classroom assessment skills so as to better detect learning problems, to teach vocabulary development, word recognition, comprehension, and text reading. In the area of reading comprehension, for example, Grade 8 teachers choose to focus on the concepts of main idea, cause and effect, summarizing, and making inferences. All teacher groups decide that sustained focus on key aspects of the required curriculum with embedded practice on complementary instructional strategies is best, so they ask for instructional coaches to work with teacher pairs for three-week sessions at a time with periodic follow-ups. With Lee's help, they find two reading coach/consultants who will work in the school over an extended period of time, ensuring continuity and avoiding mixed or conflicting messages.

The instructional coaches come on board and their interaction with teacher pairs becomes routine. Lee sees them in classrooms demonstrating and modeling strategies or observing teachers using the strategies, in the teachers' rooms critiquing the teacher's use of a strategy, or with a small group of teachers dialoguing about the best way to manage a situation in a class or solve a learning problem. Often, Lee finds one or the other coach working one-on-one with a teacher both during the class and after the class. Lee reads the coaches' integration into the faculty as an indicator that the theory of action was indeed enacted.

To be effective, action is iterative, accompanied by discovery or *reflection-in-action* (Schon, 1983). That is, while teaching, the teachers learn to ask questions about their actions and look for immediate feedback to those questions—a form of action research. The instructional consultants coach them in different questions:

- Once I identify my students' learning needs, do I know the best practices to meet those needs? What do these practices look like?
- Do I use these strategies? When and with whom?
- What do I choose to do in class and what do I ask my students to do?
- How do my students respond to my actions and requests?
- What do they actually learn?

This discovery process builds what is termed *teacher agency*, that is, creative, relevant, and situational meaning making, combined with belief that you should and can affect action and outcomes. In the taking-action phase, Lee's role is primarily one of support for teacher agency. The role includes ensuring that teachers know what best practices are and what they look like, knowing how to use them in their classrooms, nurturing an environment that fosters risk taking, and what David Cohen (1988) calls adventurous teaching. To make this happen the principal allocates the necessary resources.

Discovery can reveal additional professional development and material needs. For example, as coaches introduce new strategies and Marshall teachers begin to implement the learned strategies, they discover that they need more books for leveled reading and that the sixth-grade and seventh-grade science texts are not written at a level accessible to most of the students—this is especially true for the texts used in the ELL classes. Lee must revise budget allocations to allow purchase of these critical materials. With the new materials, teachers' enactment changes to more fully match the theory of action. Thus, enactment leads to discoveries that lead to further enactment. Lee does notice, however, that several important questions remain unanswered: For example, in what ways does student learning change as a result of these instructional changes? The time for evaluation has arrived.

STEP V OF THE INQUIRY-ACTION CYCLE: EVALUATION

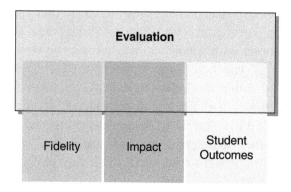

As Lee has continually demonstrated, action and inquiry go hand in hand. Now that Marshall teachers have taken action, the next step is back to inquiry in the form of evaluation. At first, the teachers (who traditionally are wary of the term evaluation) asked, "What is evaluation? Who will be evaluated? Why?" In answer, Lee defined evaluation as "an organized review of what works (and doesn't). To do so we need to look at both the process and the outcomes. Moreover, the outcomes need to be judged based on acknowledged criteria. We use what we learn to improve our future practice." Lee reiterated "This is the right thing to do, this is what professionals do—they inquire, they act, they re-inquire and re-act—for the betterment of all."

Lee described how intentional and focused evaluation requires the systematic collection of data about the processes, products, characteristics, impact, and/or outcomes of a program—meaning that they would have an opportunity to use the data they already were collecting (and possibly would continue collecting) for a new purpose. In this case, the data would be used to answer questions about the merit and worth of the professional development and the implementation of the instructional strategies in the classrooms. They would also use data to answer questions about student learning outcomes.

Lee knew that for evaluation to be a valid inquiry into the instructional improvement process, the school community beyond the teachers should be involved. An open meeting, to which interested parents and community were invited, offered a forum for evaluative deliberations. The dialogue resulted in a shared understanding that, for the Marshall community, evaluation incorporates the following elements:

- Is an ongoing process of inquiry
- Is essential to decision making

- Aims to improve the lives and work of the children, teachers, and community
- Is participatory and requires analysis and interpretation across constituency perspectives
- Generates information to be used for improving practice
- Is a continuous and repeating cycle

In summary, the community agreed that evaluation would be a tool for organizational learning and change. Evaluation activities occurred at all levels and among all instructional groups and individuals. Teachers asked important questions:

- What do we want to know and why? (Purpose)
- How will we know? (Criteria)
- Who cares? (Audience)

Lee and the teachers wanted to know if the instructional improvement efforts were working. They realized that answers to this question fell into three categories: fidelity, impact, and outcomes. First, the fidelity question: Were they really trained in state-of-the-art best practices, and were they actually implementing in their classrooms what they had learned? One of the teachers remarked on the importance of this aspect of evaluation, "I remember reading in a graduate class an article about a 'Mrs. O.' who thought she was the queen of a particular math program. She was touted as the expert in that kind of teaching. But then when the experts observed her, they saw that she was really doing her own thing—in fact her reform was no reform at all" (see Cohen, 1990).

To discover whether teachers were implementing best practices with fidelity, they agreed that Lee should schedule a few days of brief classroom instructional walk-throughs, followed by feedback debriefings with teachers whose classrooms had been observed. The teachers themselves wanted to know, "What am I actually doing and how does it compare to what I was taught? The coaches worked with me but now that they are not in my classroom, am I still doing it?"

After the first walk-through day, Lee was a bit discouraged. While the principal had expected to see differentiated instruction based on needs diagnosed through the teacher's formative assessments, what became clear was that "there is a lot of different instruction but not much differentiated instruction." However, in keeping with the definition of evaluation shared in the school, Lee's findings were integrated into the ongoing inquiry cycle. Thus, feedback informed practice, and as Lee continued the instructional walk-throughs, faithfully implemented best practices became a common sight in classrooms.

The next question centered on impact: What are the students actually doing? How does it match my instructional objectives? How do I continue to change and improve my instruction in response to what I see my students doing? To ensure that they collected enough relevant data to analyze impact on student learning, teachers explored these questions by several means. They documented their practice with brief reflective journals; they convened small groups to look at student work; and they arranged peer observations. One conversation occurred after a group had looked at eighth-grade science projects:

Marta: I don't think I have ever seen such elaborate projects—look at how the kids have produced videos, created blogs, even one interactive Web site.

Joe: I am impressed. These kids put in a lot of time and effort.

Abe: I guess you're right. But—what did they learn? Yes, the projects show they know how to do these technical things—and they are pretty glitzy. But is that what my goal was—to demonstrate their ability to create videos and such? No, I wanted them to show me they had learned relationships between gravity and mass. Do you see that in these projects? I don't think so.

In another examination of student work, sixth-grade general education teachers looked at work assigned differentially to students in an inclusive class comprised of former ELL students, children with mild learning disabilities, and nonidentified students whose first language was English. They applauded the work completed by the ELL students, noting that work with the appropriate skill levels had been assigned to each child. Several of the children with learning disabilities (LD), however, struggled with their assignments. The teachers' ensuing dialogue considered alternative modifications or possible interventions. They proposed talking with Lee about adding an extra paraprofessional in this class.

As in many of the teachers' experiences evaluating impact, these groups of teachers realized that the impact of their instruction (while "using best practice with fidelity") was not what they intended. The inquiry process brought them back to their instructional practices and to what modifications or further learning on their parts might be needed.

Finally, outcome was evaluated: Is it working? Did the students meet the curriculum goals and objectives? Lee, the teachers, and the school improvement team agreed that, as the data group had previously determined, the appropriate measures at this point were the SCAs and the MAPs. The MAP data revealed that ELL students were making gains in reading skills and appeared to be applying these skills in math and science. As they did not yet have the SCA scores for this year, this evaluation question would have to wait. Still, results on the MAPs, viewed predicatively, not diagnostically, gave them reason to be optimistic.

STEP VI OF THE INQUIRY-ACTION CYCLE: REFLECTION

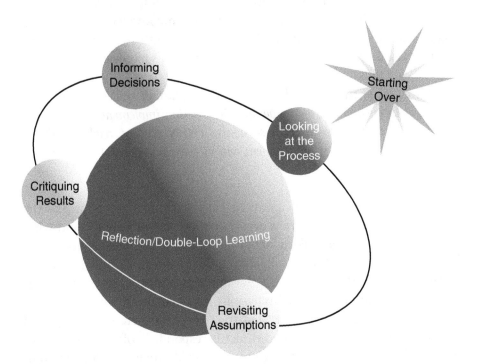

The Marshall Middle School community of practice has come full circle in this collaborative inquiry-action cycle. The last step is akin to the first step; reflection serves to start the cycle over. Lee suggested that they hold a reflection forum, so once again, faculty and staff gathered with interested business persons and parents. This time, the principal even sought out parents who appeared to be unrepresented or underrepresented at earlier gatherings. Lee made sure that parents of ELL children, children with disabilities, and parents of high achievers attended, along with the parents of noncategorized groups.

Lee opened the forum reminding the participants that this inquiry process began with the concern that *Marshall students were having trouble in core subjects and possibly with behavior because they have not mastered reading skills.* Earlier on, the school improvement team had stated the goal related to this concern as *improving learning across our diverse student body in ELA, math, and science, and reducing referrals to special education by building reading skills and comprehension.*

Next, the participants revisited the problem of practice. They determined that current instructional practice did not address the diverse and multiple needs of their students, especially ELL students and those recently exited from the ELL program, to build reading skills and be able to apply those skills in content areas. Teachers did not know how to use diagnostic data to design and/or modify instruction with strategies appropriate for various needs. Their theory of action was as follows:

> **IF** Marshall teachers build capacity for diagnosing student learning needs in reading and then modifying instruction/implementing appropriate strategies to meet those needs, **THEN** student reading will improve in all areas. Achievement will increase and referral rates will decrease.

Consensus among participants revealed sustained acceptance of the problem, so the challenge now was to review the experience and what they had learned from taking action and evaluating these actions. Had teachers' capacity to meet individual student needs within their classroom increased? Had professional development prepared them with diagnostic skills and an expanded repertoire of strategies to enable them to differentiate their instruction? Had they used the new knowledge and skills in their practice? How had students responded? Did student performance change? Did teachers continue to modify their practices based in student responses? Had the changes at Marshall Middle School improved teaching and learning? As one teacher succinctly asked, "What am I actually doing that is different, what are the results, and what am I doing with the results?"

Dialogue during the forum surfaced several discoveries:

- Not all teachers participated in coaching; not all teachers are using the learned strategies; not all classrooms have the materials and resources to implement alternative instructional strategies.

- Some teachers who worked with coaches tried some intervention and modification strategies but did not continue them long enough to see changes in student performance.
- Referrals to special education are decreasing, but only in certain classes with certain categories of students. Not all strategies work with all students, but not all teachers had learned yet how to differentiate.
- ELL teachers report remarkable progress in their students' reading skills in content areas. General education teachers whose classes contain former ELL students report feeling more confident in meeting these students' needs and have documented evidence of real learning gains.
- Teachers' anecdotes include numerous instances of collaboration, peer coaching, sharing of materials, and teaching each other new strategies.

Lee summarized the conversation:

We still have a ways to go. We may need more coaching—especially follow-up to sustain our changed practices. We need more materials. And yes, we need continued will and capacity. But I see more teachers assuming responsibility for the problems of practice and taking ownership of solutions. Teachers are making choices so their practice will profoundly engage their students. It seems to me that Marshall Middle School is now a learning organization. As such, we can reidentify our problem of practice. The issue now is not as much building capacity as it is a question of broad implementation and sustaining what we've begun.

CHAPTER SUMMARY

In Chapters 3, 4, and 5, we provided illustrative examples of the collaborative inquiry-action cycle in action. The three issues within these examples were presented in a logical and realistic sequence that is likely to occur in an improving school: coherent and aligned curriculum, useful assessments, and instructional practices. While this process is collaborative, it is unlikely to happen without the leadership of a strong principal who facilitates and focuses the work of the school and who buffers and bridges the extensive and complex environment surrounding the school. The next chapter looks at these roles necessary for a functioning collaborative inquiry-action cycle.

Questions and Exercises for Reflection and Discussion

1. How are instructional practices discussed in your school?

   - What time is set aside to discuss teaching pedagogy? Is this time honored, supported, and dedicated?
   - In what ways does the school administration monitor instructional practices?

2. What effective and meaningful professional-development opportunities exist in your school?

   - How are they determined? Do they match teachers' instructional improvement needs? Is there a process to understand teachers' instructional-improvement needs?
   - What evidence can you find that these opportunities are effective and meaningful?

3. Is instructional practice tied to the district's curriculum? If so, how is it? If not, how can this happen?

4. Are instructional approaches and strategies informed and modified by multiple sources of school data? If so, how? If not, how can this happen?

5. Use the Collaborative Action Inquiry-Action Cycle to create, review, or modify your school's instructional plan.

   - What are your **problems of practice**? How do you know this is a problem? What stakeholder groups do you have and need information from?
   - What will your plan of action look like for **acceptance**?
   - What might a **theory of action** look like in your school?
   - What is your plan of action for **taking action**? What information did you *discover*? What is the plan for *enacting* the action?
   - How will you **evaluate** what you do? What are your tools and metrics for *fidelity*, *impact*, and *outcomes*?
   - How will you ensure that the process you undertake is **reflected** upon? In what ways might the instruction in your school change as a result of this process?

PART III

Making It Happen

Roles the Inquiry-Minded, Action-Oriented Principal Plays

Lee's first year at Marshall neared its end. Changes had occurred—both in teaching and learning and in the way people interacted with each other. Most faculty members were comfortable diagnosing student needs and using instructional strategies they had learned in the various professional development activities. Teachers talking among themselves and with students about teaching and learning were a common sight. Teachers sought each other out more often for shared projects and to jointly solve problems.

So, Lee wondered, what exactly happened? The collaborative inquiry-action process appeared to be taking root at Marshall. Teaching and learning was now deeply grounded in the ongoing cycle. It had become "the way we do things here." Seldom did anyone tackle a problem or issue alone or instrumentally—that is, using the first solution that came along. Instead, people raised questions of practice that groups explored together. And Lee thought, *explore* is the operative word here. We do not seek quick and simple solutions. We've come to think outside the proverbial box, trying out ideas, even taking risks. More often than not, we both begin and end with questions—just different questions.

One thing is clear, Lee thought, I'm not working alone. We're beginning to operate as authentic communities of practice where we all bring something to the table—mutually committed to generating a solution we can all agree on. As Celia, the science teacher, e-mailed, "I've never been so involved with the core of what we are supposed to be doing in schools. I feel we have a clear purpose and the tools to do our job. Finally I am really teaching. Thank you for making it happen." But how did I make it happen? What was my role? Or, more accurately, what were my roles?

Lee thought, the principalship is not just one role—I've worn many hats to get us this far. But really, I'd say that my responsibility is to ensure that we do inquiry and act together. In that light, I have two primary roles: **facilitating and focusing** and **buffering and bridging**. One is internal; the other, externally driven. I facilitate the collaborative inquiry-action cycle; I keep it focused on teaching and learning and on fair outcomes that lead toward developing the whole child. I buffer the teams from external pressures and agenda that detract from teaching and learning; at the same time I bridge boundaries—connecting teachers and the central office, linking the school and the community.

Take today, for instance. I joined the sixth-grade math team in revising their formative assessments—I call that facilitating. I did it again, when I supported Candace's and Marco's ideas about the need to have student-level data in each marking period. I do that a lot every day. When Andy proposed "ease of administration" as the primary criteria for any test, I reminded the group that their teaching and learning goals were equally important. And I supported Benita's plea for multiple assessment that can be used across English language learner (ELL) groups. So I focused as well as facilitated.

Facilitating and focusing the inquiry-action process requires that I play other roles outside the team meetings themselves. I spent a lot of time in classrooms today. And not just for supervision—that's only a part of what I do in classrooms. Petra has been having problems with her ELL students' reading comprehension in science, so I observed a lesson, and then, while the students were working, we talked about what I saw and where she might make some adjustments. In a way, then, I am a researcher, collecting and interpreting data with teachers. I hope Petra saw me as her critical friend, raising questions of practice, more than as her supervisor. I acted as a researcher again in math; we already know some subgroups are not mastering the material, but we don't know where the problem is. So I visited a class to get a sense of what data we will need. Back in the office, I called for the breakdowns of the grade level math Marshall Assessment of Progress (MAP) scores. Together with the math team in the inquiry-action process, we'll analyze these data. I'll also have the team meet with Candace and Marco to discuss new strategies to implement, based on the data. In this way I combined my roles.

A large part of my day was filled with people who do not work in the school—so I acted as a buffer and bridger today, too. The head of the gifted and talented parents group came in early to talk about a plan to use some education foundation money to initiate an afterschool program. Then that group of parents and community folks who want to start a two-way bilingual charter school in the district met with our language coordinator and me, because they believe the charter will draw heavily from Marshall's population. They contend that the charter's existence will actually benefit us because, as they put it, we don't serve all these kids now. They say they'll be filling a gap. And Fran and I talked on the phone twice; he wanted a board presentation on the results of our recently administered school climate survey. I'm surprised at how often we are in touch—either in person or by phone or e-mail.

Today I lunched with the Rotary Club. If I expect local support for our *Writing for Work* project, I have to be out there advocating. And tomorrow I go over to make a case with the local education foundation to fund our language and literacy efforts in translating leveled books for our Somali population. I can't forget that I'm off tomorrow to the Regional Education Service Center (RESC) board meeting. There, I advocate for policies and programs that will support our goals and objectives—our theories of action. These times, I see myself as an activist.

Time to go—just enough time to grab a few minutes of dinner with my family and still get to campus on time for my university graduate class.

Marshall teachers have adapted and adopted the collaborative inquiry-action cycle because it works; it meets their needs for improving their teaching and student learning in their classrooms. Similarly, relevant and involved community members participate because they see benefits for themselves and the community's children. It is often said that success breeds success. In this case, as educators and community members were able to *see* how their efforts were realized in student learning, they became even more eager to continue the process, to look for the *next* problem of practice to identify and address. But, why were they willing to engage in the process initially? What led them to believe it would work?

Answering these questions makes evident the crucial roles the principal plays. An inquiry-minded, action-oriented principal *facilitates* the process as well as the teachers' willingness to be involved. As facilitator, this principal also keeps the *focus* of the inquiry on practice. This practice focus is relentless and laserlike on the school's core technology: *Instructional practices to impact student learning.* The focus also emphasizes that learning is both cognitive and affective, involving the whole child and preparing the child to be a productive citizen. Lee assumes a role in the communities of practice akin to that of the Speaker of the House in Congress, whose primary duty is less to vote than to set an agenda. For the principal, the agenda is to bring attention, necessary support, and resources to the core technology of schooling; that is, to facilitate and focus the work of schooling. To keep the school community centered on what is important, an inquiry-minded, action-oriented principal also *buffers and bridges.* This means that principals like Lee use their knowledge of the education system and the forces within the community to protect and support the core technology; at the same time, they span boundaries, translating what happens outside the school and advocating for what is happening inside. These principals know that these complex dual roles allow teachers and other staff to center their efforts, maintain motivation in the face of adversity and distractions, and obtain resources for continuous improvement. This chapter elaborates what an inquiry-minded, action-oriented principal actually does while facilitating and focusing and buffering and bridging.

THE FACILITATOR AND FOCUSER

A successful collaborative inquiry-action cycle requires that teachers take ownership of their teaching and the challenges associated with it—and at the same time, the cycle makes possible such ownership. Teacher ownership and teacher leadership go hand in hand. Principals facilitate teacher leadership by developing a school culture that can effectively implement the collaborative inquiry-action cycle. Consequently, principals are facilitators and focusers who create the conditions that support the important work of teachers and other staff. As facilitators and focusers, they integrate the diverse perspectives, needs, and forces present in their schools; they seek coherence. They shape and maintain an environment of teacher empowerment; they provide sustained, meaningful, and effective professional development; they motivate teachers; they create legitimate time and content for communities of collaborative practice; they nurture a culture of high expectations for all students; they reward and celebrate accomplishments; they share and model effective practice; they mobilize resources for curricular and instructional improvements; they are inclusive of multiple cultural perspectives; they actively recruit and retain a diverse body of teachers; and they dismiss ineffective teachers.

Such principals place steady and relentless pressure on the center of the target, that is, the core technology of teaching and learning (see the following figure). These principals also have to facilitate this focus within and outside their school community. The facilitator and focuser asks educators to keep a constant eye on both the target of student learning and their own practice. This is not easy. The principal asks educators to keep their head on a swivel; to constantly look around—inwardly at their practice and outwardly to accomplishments of student learning. As a result, being a facilitator and focuser is lived by a principal who accomplishes several tasks:

- Motivating teacher will
- Building teacher capacity

- Establishing collaborative and participatory decision-making processes
- Making research-based, information-rich decisions
- Monitoring, recognizing, and rewarding practice and learning

Motivating Teacher Will

What one believes contributes to what one does. That is, belief feeds action. However, the reciprocal is also true; that is, action feeds belief. As a result, an inquiry-minded, action-oriented principal must build teachers' will to either believe in or engage in new practices. Building will is a matter of motivation. For a principal to motivate teachers to engage in new, different practices they will have to help the teacher build agency; that is, take ownership. Agency does not constitute the often futile struggle to get others to think differently (beliefs), because agency can be developed through actions. Specifically, the principal must press for changes in practice. Leithwood and Steinbach (1991) found that, to motivate such changes, highly effective principals worked with groups of teachers on the

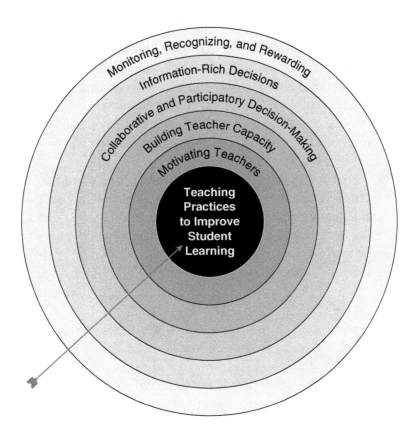

following three issues: (1) developing better solutions to problems, (2) stimulating commitment to defensible goals, and (3) promoting long-term problem-solving skills. Simultaneously, principals must sustain teachers' attention on student learning (Elmore, Peterson, and McCarthy, 1996).

While teaching practices and student learning are at the core of actions, beliefs should not be dismissed. While actions may transform beliefs, there are also core beliefs that all educators must exhibit, including high expectations for all students, adherence to agreed upon curricular standards, equalized opportunities, and righteous and inclusive educational goals. Motivating teachers is not an explicitly taught skill in most preservice principal-preparation programs. However, principals can attest that once in the job, motivation is a critical ingredient in the principal role of facilitator and focuser.

Building Teacher Capacity

Effective leaders devote considerable time to supporting teachers in their efforts to strengthen the quality of instruction. They help teachers build the necessary knowledge and skills to perform their jobs effectively; they build teacher capacity. Their support takes various forms. For example, inquiry-minded, action-oriented principals make sure that teachers have all the necessary support (e.g., materials) and resources (e.g., financial, technological) required to be highly effective instructors. They also draw on their schools' social and human capital to provide access to new sources of knowledge and make certain that teachers have high-quality opportunities to expand, enhance, and refine their instructional skills (Murphy, 2001). Thus, professional development is critical, and principals play a key role in both planning and delivering professional development to teachers.

Professional development and learning is an ongoing process embedded throughout the school. Teachers who are professionals are dedicated to building and improving their knowledge base and skills—their expertise—in curricular content and pedagogy. They seek opportunities for ongoing professional learning and development, for themselves and for the entire organization (see Darling-Hammond & Sykes, 1999). Principals help provide teachers with such professional development opportunities that are aligned with the schools' identified needs and goals.

Studies conducted on the effectiveness of professional development opportunities for teachers provide insight about both the content and the manner of instruction to make professional development experiences beneficial to teachers. Professional development matters to instruction more than mere curricular or standard changes (Ball & Cohen, 1999).

Inquiry-minded, action-oriented principals create professional development opportunities that exhibit the following characteristics:

- Centered on matters of instruction (Ball & Cohen, 1999)
- Collaboration (Abdal-Haag, 1998; Ball & Cohen, 1999; Blase & Blase, 1998; Lieberman & Miller, 1999; Little, 1993; Putnam & Borko, 2000; Rosenholtz, 1989)
- Subject specificity (Ball & Cohen, 1999; Hawley & Valli, 1999; Sykes, 1999; Wilson & Berne, 1999)
- Site specific (Joyce & Showers, 1988)
- Ongoing—not a one-time workshop (Joyce & Showers, 1988)

Affirming the above, Porter, Garet, Desimone, and Birman (2003) have found consistent empirical support for the following characteristics of effective professional development experiences:

- The content focus of the activity, such as the degree to which the activity enhances teachers' content knowledge and supports how students learn the content
- The duration of the activity, including the total number of hours that participants spend in it, as well as the span of time over which the activity takes place
- The degree to which the activity includes the collective participation of teachers from the same school, department, or grade level
- The extent to which the activity offers opportunities for the participants' active learning
- The coherence of the activity, that is, consistency of the teachers' professional development with other activities, and its alignment with the appropriate standards and assessments

Inquiry-minded, action-oriented principals also ensure that teachers have appropriate guidance as they work to integrate skills learned during professional development into their instructional behaviors (Berman & McLaughlin, 1978). By supporting and developing a school context and culture for teacher learning through collaboration and support, principals have a profound impact on teacher professional development (Gamoran & Grodsky, 2003).

Perhaps most importantly, effective professional development is driven by analyses of student performance. Hawley and Valli (2007) stated, "Such analyses will define what educators need, rather than want, to learn, make professional development student-centered, and increase public confidence in the use of resources for professional development"

(p. 120). Involving teachers in both the identification of the content and the design of the learning opportunities enhances their commitment and motivation. Thus, building capacity and will through professional development opportunities requires attention to collaboration, participation, and the use of data.

Establishing Collaborative and Participatory Decision-Making Processes

By creating collaborative and participatory decision making experiences, inquiry-minded, action-oriented principals facilitate the school faculty's examination of teaching and learning in the school. When engaged and provided with rewarding experiences in which they can be successful, teachers feel efficacious and are motivated to take on leadership roles and become active participants in their schools. Leaders play a crucial role in establishing a culture with mutual respect and participatory governance. They realize that communities of professional practice require resources as well, and they take advantage of their unique position to garner and allocate resources to bring communities of professional practice to life (DuFour, Eaker, & DuFour, 2005; Little, 1982a; Printy, 2008).

Research indicates that school leaders support integrated communities of practice through providing the infrastructure that nurtures a professional learning atmosphere for teachers (Marks & Printy, 2003; Printy, 2008). This infrastructure includes providing and legitimatizing the necessary time and space to meet and make meaningful decisions. While time is an overused, confounding variable or inhibitor to change, legitimate time (focused on content, data, and solutions; resourced with school day time and space; supported and attended by all stakeholders) can formally nurture a collaborative, participatory, decision making process that is meaningful and, in the end, effective. Providing legitimate time and space can also nurture informal learning throughout the school (see Little, 1982b; Newmann, King, & Rigdon, 1997; Reeves, 2004; Schmoker, 1999). The inquiry-minded, action-oriented principal uses the cycle as a framework of support for cultures of learning and professional behavior.

Making Research-Based, Information-Rich Decisions

A U.S. Department of Education (2002) report stated that education continues to operate "largely on the basis of ideology and professional consensus. As such, it is subject to fads and is incapable of cumulative progress that follows from the application of the scientific method and from the systemic collection and use of objective information" (p. 48). The reaction to such claims is the clear and present (and sanctioned) press to make decisions on problems "uncovered by empirical data and . . . programs proven effective by research to raise student achievement" (Massell, 2001, p. 148).

As a result, the inquiry-minded, action-oriented principal must become a consumer of input and output data. Input data include current research findings on best practices. The principal must be agile with the data, making sure that the data set is complete, that the research-based practices have merit, and that local context and agreed-upon local goals are attended to. Only then can the principal transform data into meaningful information and knowledge for teachers and connect teachers to proven practices. While data are difficult to use in the practice of educating youth, data can inform our knowledge of pedagogy and student learning; therefore, data can have a positive impact on teaching and learning.

Consequently, understanding how raw data are contextualized into usable information and then transformed into new knowledge for teaching is important for effective school principals (Earl & Katz, 2002; O'Day, 2002; Petrides & Nodine, 2003). Rather than seeing data as valuable as an end point, inquiry-minded, action-oriented principals think in terms of how data become knowledge. Petrides and Guiney (2002, p. 1711) indicate that a knowledge management framework brings together the organizational resources of people, processes, and technologies and is anchored in four principles:

1. Evaluating the current available information

2. Determining information needed to support decision making

3. Operating within the context and perspective of the school's organizational processes

4 Assessing the school's information culture and politics

This process moves from the typical focus on one set of student achievement data (typically summative state assessments) toward a process of reflection that includes both inquiry and action.

To illustrate that the knowledge management framework is more than the mere collection and application of data, we draw on an example from the World Health Organization (WHO). Choo (2001) analyzed the WHO smallpox eradication program of the late 1960s. He concluded that the program melded together the elements of sense making, knowledge creation, and decision making "into continuous cycles of interpretation, innovation, and adaptive action" (p. 202). Rather than focus on program input data (i.e., the number of vaccinations), "information gathering was comprehensive, involving participants at all levels of the program, including local villagers and community leaders" (p. 204). Choo determined that the eradication of smallpox by 1977 in Somalia was more a triumph of effective information management than of the technology of medicine itself. In the end, the process-oriented and culturally centered approach provides promising leads to the utilization of student learning data in schools.

Data-based and evidenced-based practices are at the core of any inquiry cycle. Principals must play a key role in both understanding and using data and research practices themselves and also in helping others to embrace and use data-based or information-rich practices. Principals collaboratively use information to identify a problem of practice; they gather multiple sets of data; they generate new data; they analyze and transform data into meaningful information; they transform this information into knowledge that can be used to make scientifically based programmatic, and pedagogical improvements; they evaluate the impact of strategies aimed at the problem of practice; and they revisit past and present problems of practice. These principals are analytic knowledge builders.

In this role, data-based decision making knowledge is part of the repertoire for school principals. They facilitate teachers' use of data in order to identify individual student needs so they can tailor instruction, provide remedial assistance, assign or reassign students to classes or groups, and find and correct gaps in the curriculum. Furthermore, data can be used to identify areas where teachers need to strengthen their own content knowledge or teaching skills—in other words, where to direct professional development.

In response to and monitoring the work of the inquiry-action cycle, data can drive school-wide strategic plans and resource allocation. Data become information to evaluate policies and programs and to develop and improve curriculum, teaching, and learning. These data are used to continually guide improvement, and thus are not an end-of-the-year occurrence. Through the inquiry-action cycle, principals encourage teachers and other participants to use multiple types and sources of data to understand the school's strengths and weaknesses, set priorities, focus change efforts, and establish a baseline from which to monitor progress. In this way, data use becomes an important lever for creating and supporting professional relationships in schools resulting in collective, organizational learning.

School leaders today must have expertise in how to transform the glut of data at their disposal into meaningful information that they can use to facilitate and focus school practice. Wayman and Stringfield (2006) describe this as "the paradoxical situation of being both data rich and information poor" (p. 464). Nonetheless, "data provide a ready-made vehicle for engaging staff in planning. Leaders can broaden the base of inquiry by distributing leadership and developing a cadre of people which is competent and confident with using data" (Earl & Katz, 2002, p. 1020). Inquiry-minded, action-oriented principals can transform data into information through the use of the collaborative inquiry-action cycle. In turn, the cycle itself facilitates a focus on data-driven issues and inspires the development of new knowledge and actions in an information-rich environment.

Monitoring, Recognizing, and Rewarding Practice and Learning

Principals' facilitation and focusing also occurs in the classroom as they attend to the practice of teaching and learning: They lead and manage by walking around; they engage in curricular and pedagogical work directly with teachers; they share and model effective instruction for teachers; they monitor policies and standards; they are highly visible; they hear from students regarding learning; they monitor instruction; and they are attuned to the pulse and the undercurrents of the school. This role enacted brings the term instructional leadership to life.

In the first chapter, we highlighted findings from a meta-analysis of principal behaviors that led to systemic school change and student learning gains. The meta-analysis also highlights the importance of principals' situational awareness, visibility, contingent rewards, monitoring and evaluating, and affirmation. Effective principals also demonstrate personal interest in staff and make themselves available (Marzano, Waters, & McNulty, 2005).

The challenge in schools is to facilitate and focus attention on teaching and learning with a group. While studying the actions of the individual has been historically difficult, our knowledge is "Babylonian when it comes to groups" (Homans, 1950, p. 4). Homans's studies of the Hawthorne Work at the Western Electric Company in Chicago, between 1927 and 1932, revealed that motivation is centered on activity (what workers do), sentiment (what workers feel), and interaction (relationships with one another). As a result, leaders must attend to all three facets. The collaborative inquiry-action cycle attends to each of these elements.

The facilitator and focuser attends to motivating teachers' will, building teacher capacity, establishing collaborative and participatory decision making processes, making information-rich decisions, and monitoring, recognizing, and rewarding practice and learning. However, this alone is not a recipe for success. In fact, such efforts will be subsumed if trapped in a dysfunctional organization.

Elmore (2003b) argues that policies with stakes in incoherent organizations do not cause the organizations to become more coherent and effective:

> The stakes are mediated and refracted by the organizations on which they fall. Stakes, if they work at all, do so by mobilizing resources, capacities, knowledge, and competencies that, by definition, are not present in the organizations and individuals whom they are intended to affect. (p. 288)

Because of the power of what lies outside the schoolhouse doors, we next explore the need for the inquiry-minded, action-oriented principal to act as the buffer and bridger.

THE BUFFER AND BRIDGER

The world outside the schoolhouse can be both positive and supportive or negative and disruptive. Schools are not bound to a single community or a single neighborhood. As organizations, schools operate within a larger environment of systems: the district and other governmental agencies and departments, the surrounding neighborhood and the larger community, and overall political and social institutions. The forces of these various external systems on the school create an "organization in a loosely coupled state" (Meyer & Rowan, 1991, p. 60). Simply put, within schools, some elements (typically the managerial functions) are tightly linked, while others (such as teaching and learning) are loosely linked, allowing degrees of freedom in practice implementation. At the same time, links to other organizations vary in strength outside the school across the larger system; some demands or influences cannot be ignored while others are easily discounted.

Historically, this looseness in connections across and within systems actually served to facilitate internal freedom of action by buffering the impact of outside forces (Thompson, 1967). However, daily practice still suffers from lack of coherence and from the inefficiencies of unclear and unshared goals and technologies. The decoupling of structures and activities in schools has made rules, regulations and rituals more important than professional and collaborative decision making, communication, and action (Meyer & Rowan, 1991). This perspective highlights the need for the bridging and buffering role of the school principal.

Principals serve to shield those inside the school from negative and disruptive forces at the same time they span the boundaries of the schoolhouse, importing valuable and necessary resources. A key role for principals, then, in implementing the inquiry-action cycle is buffering and bridging within and across the system and throughout the community. The inquiry-minded, action-oriented principal is successful when the buffer and bridger sides of the role are in balance (see the following figure).

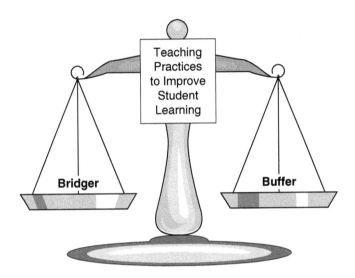

A school is not an island, operating in isolation. Managing the school within its environment is, indeed, a balancing act for the principal. Because a school cannot do everything and respond effectively to all external demands, principals make choices regarding the interdependencies, interrelationships, and interactions between the school and its environmental context. They use various organizational design strategies to coordinate with their communities as well as strategic maneuvering to alter or broaden their environments, thus giving the school some control over what they do inside (Kotter, 1979; Pfeffer & Salancik, 1978). They also rely on various buffering strategies to protect the school from external influences and interference, thus reducing uncertainties and interdependencies (Galbraith, 1977; Thompson, 1967). Principals operate the bridge in both directions; they carry the messages outward and bring the external resources in. They also choose to close the bridge at times when people, programs, and processes inside need protection.

While principals, other school leaders, and teachers have an important role in the education of students, the community and home environment have an equal—possibly even greater—impact on student learning. Both community agencies and the home have mutual and deep investments in the lives of students. It falls to principals to manage the interconnections between the school and community. Principals also establish the community as the context for the learning process—recognizing that learning is rooted in the experiences, diversity, and history of the local community. Principals are in a position to act as environmental leaders, "operating in the community outside their schools while also bringing the community into their schools" (Goldring & Sullivan, 1996, p. 207).

A principal's management of the environment may start with the school's work with parents, guardians, and families. Increasingly, families in communities come from a range of social classes, races, and ethnic backgrounds, bringing a corresponding range of values and cultural norms that influence school performance. Principals find themselves honoring and integrating this mix into a functioning whole that is the school community, so that it can serve as an anchor for the larger community. They bridge through fostering family involvement, and they buffer by setting reasonable and acceptable parameters around that involvement (see Epstein, 2001; Lareau, 2000).

Effective schools are characterized as providing opportunities for parents to both support and participate in their children's education (Smith & O'Day, 1991). Principals want parent involvement because it has such positive benefits for students, families, and schools, including academic achievement (see Henderson, Mapp, Johnson, & Davies, 2007; Hoover-Dempsey & Sandler, 1997). Parent or family involvement can include school-based activities, such as attending parent-teacher conferences and volunteering in the classroom, as well as home-based activities, such as helping with homework, reading with the student at home and talking about school matters. An elementary school offers an example of a proactive organizational redesign aimed at bringing in parents by establishing a parents' library within the school's library. Similarly, many urban schools provide a parents' room or lounge where they may hold meetings, learn of events or available resources, or simply grab a cup of coffee while waiting for their child or to speak with a teacher. Many schools offer strategic activities for parents to be a regular part of classroom (e.g., weekly volunteer opportunities in the classroom with specific, assigned roles). Principals balance these open-door activities by setting and disseminating clear terms for how parents can enter or communicate with individuals in the school. For example, many schools today have locked doors, and few schools allow unrestricted access to classrooms; visitors must at least check in at the front office. Schools develop e-mail or phone protocols for teacher-parent communication that protect teachers' time while still encouraging access.

Another dimension of school-community relationships is much broader than parents, guardians, and families. To assert that schools by themselves can address the multiple challenges facing students in today's society would be foolish. Few schools have such capacity, especially as pivotal indicators of social and economic well-being continue to decline. Furthermore, what we know about how children learn suggests that communities should be much more closely connected to teaching and learning; linking in-school learning to real-world contexts in which such knowledge must be used is essential to learning (Wehlage, Newmann, & Secada, 1996). Productive school-community relationships occur when educators better understand the nonschool environments in which students function (Bransford, Brown, & Cocking, 2000). Communities not only provide the structures that facilitate learning but they also shape and determine what learning is valued.

Thus, inquiry-minded, action-oriented principals recognize and understand out-of-school contexts and the importance of the nonschool learning communities that shape students' understandings. They work to create *school as community* and *community as school*, establishing real connections that bring agencies and services into the school building while supporting ways for children to learn in community venues outside the school. The balancing act again requires strategies that redesign the school, maneuver the environment, and reduce interference.

One redesign strategy principals use is to bring professionals into the school—but not everyone, just the right ones. They guide service providers, youth development specialists, and private organizations to create opportunities in the schoolhouse to serve children with multiple and varying needs (Manswell Butty, LaPoint, Thomas, & Thompson, 2001). For example, many principals create links with social service agencies to relocate service providers inside the school; thus, community health nurses, mental health practitioners, law enforcement personnel, nutrition counselors, optometrists, and dentists are common sights in many schools. As a result, more kids are ready to learn because they feel safe, eat well, can see the board, and have their physical and emotional needs met. Another area where principals employ redesign is in special education services; principals who support inclusive classrooms often rearrange schedules and teaching assignments to reconfigure classrooms to function for more than one professional adult.

Still, principals also have to establish reasonable boundaries to protect learning from harmful, miscellaneous, and irrelevant distractions. Principals filter in what is important and filter out what is not. One principal tells of rejecting the fluoride company's offer to provide mouthwash for daily rinsing, led by the morning classroom teachers: "I chose to act as a gatekeeper. Time spent getting ready to rinse, rinsing, and cleaning up after rinsing is time away from learning. Some distractions from time-on-task are definitely worthwhile. Rinsing with fluoride is not."

Similarly, principals buffer their faculty from distractions through their choices to allocate or reallocate resources. For example, they may choose to outsource mundane tasks such as lunch or recess duty. One principal reports contracting a temp agency to input schedules so that counselors can concentrate on working directly with kids and teachers to support instruction and learning. Another principal enacted a different form of outsourcing, including partnering with local mental health agencies to free school counselors of duties they were not trained to conduct (Militello, Schweid, & Carey, 2008). This example combines elements of the principal as buffer and bridger.

Principals are also responsible for strategic maneuvering efforts that advocate for the school, carrying the message of the faculty and students out into relevant places in the community, such as foundations or businesses. This approach can link learning activities to community activities, such as supporting teachers who seek opportunities for off-site instruction. One middle school principal helped the eighth-grade team to arrange partnerships with the local lumber yard, hardware store, and carpenter to allow students to participate in the real work of building tables for the new youth center. This same principal opposed random field trips to local historical sites: "If kids leave the building during the day, it is to learn something they cannot learn here, with their families, or by themselves. Field trips do not fit that category."

Advocating may also mean newly articulating the school's mission so that it is powerful and can be taken to foundations or regional corporations to promote school purposes and activities and to garner support. By speaking at a public forum or addressing civic organizations, principals develop civic capacity with key institutions and organizations in the community (Goldring & Hausman, 2001). Subsequent support may be symbolic or financial, but either serves to bring some form of resource into the schoolhouse. Principals seek to develop and disseminate images that influence external perceptions and knowledge about the school. The projected image says, *This is who we are, and what we stand for is good. Support us.* Inquiry-minded, action-oriented principals use the collaborative inquiry-action cycle to build these exportable messages and images through articulating theories of action. Often they invite relevant community members to participate in the cycle.

Finally, bridging and buffering includes advocating for and implementing ethical education policies that support teaching and learning (see Rallis, Rossman, Cobb, Reagan, & Kuntz, 2008). Principals reach out to ensure that external policy initiatives serve their students and their families. They make choices to protect their schools from mindless bureaucratic implementation of policies that constantly come at schools from numerous sources: international bodies, national governments, states, districts, and of course, local practices. The buffering may require adaptation before adoption of a policy or even wholesale rejection of a policy initiative the principal judges to be inappropriate or unjust. For example, some principals may choose to adapt the English language learner laws in their states for implementation that fits the local context. Others use discretion in the degrees with which they implement NCLB.

CHAPTER SUMMARY

This chapter reveals what an inquiry-minded, action-oriented principal does to draw members of the school community into the communities of practice that enact inquiry cycles. We describe and illustrate the roles these principals play: They *facilitate and focus*; and they *buffer and bridge*. We show how in the first role, the principal aims to motivate teachers' will and build teachers' capacities; establish collaborative and participatory decision-making processes, ensure that decisions are research-based and information-rich, and monitor, recognize, and reward practice and learning. We present buffering and bridging as a balancing act for inquiry-minded, action-oriented principals. The role entails work throughout the school community: crafting an environment that supports the technical core of the school, high-quality instruction, promulgating high expectations for both teaching and for student learning, allocating and reallocating resources, ensuring safety, breaking down barriers that impede student learning, elevating the status of good teachers, providing a diverse set of educational opportunities, and challenging the system.

Finally, as facilitators and focusers, buffers and bridgers, principals are *stewards of the public good*. Principals buffering efforts protect the school people and their work from external distractions and forces that can influence or drive decisions toward special interests or even inhibit efforts toward intended ethical outcomes; at the same time, their focusing efforts center the schools' vision and actions on achieving these righteous outcomes. We see these roles not only as socially just but also as doable and realistic. While we have described the roles as separate, they are integrated and overlapping. Recognizing these roles as such reduces the complexity of the job. The principal's facilitation and bridging bring all the forces together into a coherent, working whole that mindfully inquires, acts, and reflects on these actions collaboratively across the community. These are the roles that principals like Lee must play to accomplish the collaborative inquiry-action cycle.

Questions and Exercises for Reflection and Discussion

1. Thinking about principals you know, select an instance where they have played one of the roles described in this chapter.

   - What did they do to illustrate the role?
   - What were the circumstances?
   - Were they comfortable?
   - How could the role have been played differently to be more effective?

2. Which roles do you believe you are strong in enacting?

3. Which roles do you believe you need additional development in? How might you go about improving the skills required in these roles?

4. An exercise at the end of Chapters 3, 4, and 5 asked you to develop details for each step of the collaborative inquiry-action cycle. Using one of these plans, create a simulation with other current or aspiring principals to understand the roles you need to play to implement the plan. After the simulation, discuss when different roles were needed for moving the work forward.

You Can Do It!

Putting the Collaborative Inquiry-Action Cycle Into Practice

One of Lee's professional activities was to serve on the board of the regional education service center (RESC). At the June meeting, the conversation turned to the success Lee and two other principals demonstrated in raising student achievement, including scores on the State Comprehensive Assessment (SCA). Danny Santos, the RESC director, asked what they thought accounted for the improvement: "How did you do it?" Ayesha Petrie, principal of a large and diverse high school, and Marcus Drew, an elementary principal, joined Lee in responding. All three principals led schools that were recently rated as high performing.

Lee answered first. "It took collaboration. Inquiry. Action. Reflection and more inquiry. It's a cycle. In fact, I've been able to break it down into steps. We start with identifying the problem and then ensuring that everyone involved accepts it as our problem. Then we establish the goal we will be responsible for and how we will reach that goal—we call that our *theory of action*. That's the inquiry part; next comes the action. We've learned not to stop there. We examine our actions and decide what needs to be strengthened or changed. The Marshall Middle School family calls it the collaborative inquiry-action cycle."

Ayesha nodded. "Sounds like the process we use. We don't call it that though. And we emphasize that last part, the reflection—to us reflection means thinking *and* doing, so I guess we are talking about the same things."

"Sounds familiar to me, too. I like your name for it because that is what school improvement is all about—inquiry and action. Working together," said Marcus.

"What makes this cycle so special?" Danny asked.

Lee answered, "It's collaborative. We work together."

Marcus added, "And it took our commitment to improving instruction."

"Everything we did was based on practice—what we are actually doing in the school," said Ayesha.

"The school wasn't doing it alone. I'm just thinking about all the outside resources we drew on through the cycle," said Lee.

"Having a framework to guide us is important. As Lee said, it is a cycle, so it's not prescriptive. It's a process."

"For the cycle to work, you have to remember that context matters. How we go through the process in my school is likely to be quite different from your process," said Marcus. "And not just because my school is elementary and yours are not. The kids, the parents, and the communities are different."

"So was it easy?" asked Danny.

"In a way, yes, because I did not have to do it all alone. My faculty, parents, and often community members were at my side: Defining problems of practice, articulating goals and how we would get there, doing it—and then evaluating and reflecting. And repeating this cycle as we saw the need."

"But honestly, I faced a lot of challenges," said Ayesha. "I had to adapt the framework a lot. Contexts change. And people resist change. They resist reflection, too."

"I agree. The cycle rolls out different every time. So we have to be nimble," said Marcus. "And the teachers have to be nimble. I'd say that success of the cycle hinges on teachers being leaders."

Ayesha added, "I like that, being *nimble*. Makes me realize how much the cycle supports my learning. I need to always be a learner. If I'm not growing, how can I expect it of others? This process of the cycle really forces me to examine and reexamine constantly. I ask, 'Is this working? And how do I know it is working?'"

Finally, Danny asked, "What can we tell other principals? Aspiring principals? District leaders? Professors? Professional development providers?"

"That you can do this—that you can improve teaching and learning in your school." The three principals answered almost simultaneously.

The faculty, staff, and leadership in these three turnaround schools did more than express beliefs that their students could achieve. They acted to increase achievement. All three schools have adapted and adopted the collaborative inquiry-action cycle because it works. Through this process, school educators took on a new way of thinking. The changes are systemic, enduring, and meaningful.

In Piagetian terms, they accommodated their schema, not merely assimilated short-term adherence to ideas (see Piaget, 1985). They moved from a stable state through disequilibrium toward a new stability—until the process began again. The school community members were learners all. The cycle leveraged teachers' "hearts, minds, and practices" (Elmore, 2003a, p. 204). Thinking changed; practices changed; results changed.

At the beginning of this book, we debunked the myth of the great principal while maintaining that positive change requires leadership of an inquiry-minded, action-oriented principal. We offered the collaborative inquiry-action cycle as a tool for learning and change. The cycle serves as a framework to shape and guide an inclusive and ongoing process that can become the school culture, *the way we do things here* (Bolman & Deal, 2008). Engaging in the cycle is more about changing norms, habits, skills, and beliefs than about changing formal structures. It is about organizational learning, and at the heart of organizational learning is the ability to enter into a professional community, to develop modes of inquiry, and to take risks. The learning process works because the cycle:

- Is collaborative
- Is iterative with ebb and flow across the steps
- Focuses on the core technology of teaching and learning
- Is based on concrete practices
- Harnesses community support and resources
- Recognizes teachers as leaders

Of course, challenges exist to impede initiation of the cycle as well as maintaining and sustaining its ongoing practice. Multiple challenges lie in the contextual variable of each setting. Others lie in human resistance to change.

WHAT IT TAKES

Collaboration is the linchpin of the cycle. To accomplish improvement, principals do not inquire and act alone. They invite; they include; they create opportunities for engagement. They are willing to relinquish control to gain participation and ownership on the part of the community. This local network may include any of the following groups: teachers; other school personnel; parents; people from community government, agencies, and business; local foundations; and entrepreneurs. Collaboration means teamwork, partnerships, alliances; it also means negotiation, conciliation, compromises, and other forms of give and take. Most important, effective collaboration requires dialogue that produces new ways of thinking.

Through dialogue, collaboration results in learning; learners need "access to communities of learning, interpretation, exploration, and knowledge" (Brown & Duguid, 2000, p. 232). The cycle provides for such a community of learning and thus for shared responsibility for action. As Lee explained, "I think what makes the difference is that everyone seems willing to take responsibility for meeting the goals we set, for taking the necessary actions. They accept the problems as theirs, not as belonging to some abstract, disembodied force." As principal, Lee plays the roles that are necessary to make collaboration possible—and ensure that collaboration balances both inquiry and action.

True collaboration with authentic dialogue builds the trust necessary for participants to open up to each other and take limited risks in their practice. Being part of a community of practice that engages in the cycle means spending long hours of dedicated time addressing substantive issues; the time spent is worthwhile because the result is action, not just talk. As people in the group spend more and more time with each other in the cycle, they come to agree on and share common goals. They also see that their ideas are respected and no recriminations or sanctions result from disagreements. Instead, new understandings develop as alternative perspectives and agendas are aired. This safety and mutual commitment to common ends serve as a solid foundation for developing genuine trust necessary to change practices for improvement.

Another linchpin of the cycle is the tight focus on the core technology, namely, teaching practices to impact student learning. Innovations cannot be regulated to the periphery of schools (see Cohen, 1988). That is, reforms must be embedded in the core technology of schooling—teaching and learning. The further out the reform is from the core of schools, the less effect it will have. "The problem is finding structures that reflect and reinforce competing theories of good teaching and learning" (Sykes & Elmore, 1988, p. 84) instead of buffering and marginalizing aspects of instruction from reform efforts. The collaborative inquiry-action cycle is such a structure that moves the school toward becoming a coherent system focused on improving its core technology.

The power of the cycle is that it drives action. Its focus is concrete reality, not some abstract ideal. The cycle can grab people by their practice, as Elmore (2002a) directs. Talk is fine but may lead nowhere; action with evaluation and reflection produces movement. As Marshall demonstrates, through the cycle, curriculum is aligned; formative assessments are created, administered, and used to diagnose problems; and instructional strategies are expanded and improved. Schools don't need years and years of culture building; they need inquiry and action, which in turn generates risk taking, standards-based practices, and ultimately a new culture.

The real triggers of school improvement continue to be good teaching and student motivation, not punitive accountability measures. First and foremost, the cycle fosters good teaching; its tight focus on instructional practice and results combined with the embedded professional learning builds capacity for teacher as professionals. Being a professional means possessing and using a disciplined body of knowledge to meet the needs of the clients.

At the same time the cycle builds professional capacity, it serves as a positive accountability mechanism. In the absence of internal defined and monitored accountability, external (and often punitive) mechanisms will be created to fill the void. With active inquiry-action cycles fully functioning, the school community can account for strengths, weaknesses, accomplishments, and efforts toward improvement. The school can take responsibility for accountability, balancing internal and external needs and demands regarding teaching and learning.

The iterative aspect, the ebb and flow, of the cycle is crucial for learning. No one is locked into a determined sequence searching for predetermined answers. Instead, the cycle allows for flexibility, for taking risks and making mistakes—and for correcting them. It recognizes the "Ready, Fire, Aim" (Fullan, 1993, p. 31) mentality in schools, providing opportunities to "re-aim" before firing again, this time with new knowledge and with the target more directly in view. The cycle supports Elmore's (1979, 1983) backward-mapping design, which begins with the end in mind as a means to support activity at the delivery level. This back and forth allows for redefining the end and where to begin. This process matches the constant and persistent attention to both inquiry and action offered in this book. For example, the cycle encouraged Marshall's faculty to see assessments as more than simply raw data or end points. They chose to use assessments harmoniously and interactively, at the beginning (diagnostic), middle (formative), and end (summative judgments), thus marrying inquiry and action.

Just as the cycle cannot be effective if done by the principal alone, the school cannot address all problems of practice alone. Consequently, inquiry-minded, action-oriented principals harness community support and resources. They seek out partnerships that embed community resources in the school and that are closer to the student clientele. If we want changes in our world, then schools must look to the worlds in which they sit. As schools bring in the children of the community, they must also bring in the community's resources and support—time, talent, materials, and money. As discussed earlier, these principals see *schools as community* and *community in schools*. Paradoxically, the way to move forward may be "to look around" (Brown & Duguid, 2000, p. 8).

Looking around must also include looking within at one of the school's most valuable resources, its teachers. Therefore, the cycle values and honors those who do the day-to-day work of teaching and learning—namely, teachers. Participation recognizes them as leaders and increases individual agency. To engage in the cycle means building professional capacity. Teachers, as professionals, understand the complexities of learning, and they seek new ways to improve their knowledge and skills to better serve the students in their schools. They have experienced the continually moving targets of education reform. They often recognize that their students' needs cannot be met within the confines of their classrooms; consequently, their work naturally extends beyond the classroom. Moreover, they have the skills, expertise, and will to be powerful agents of change. However, they have seldom found avenues for empowerment without leaving the teaching ranks. The collaborative inquiry-action cycle uses teachers' skill, expertise, and experience to position them as leaders. Spillane, Halverson, and Diamond (2001) describe distributed leadership as a practice "*stretched over* the school's social and situational context" (p. 23; italics in original), embedded within activities. The cycle provides a vehicle that stretches leadership to engage teachers as experts interacting with each other around concrete tasks and activities. Here, teachers can be leaders without becoming administrators or taking on quasi-administrative roles.

As leaders, these teachers have a new, systemic vantage point on instruction and school improvement. When teachers step out of the isolation imposed by the "egg-carton" structure of schools (Lortie, 1975), they question and challenge practices that they recognize as ineffective in and across classrooms. Through the collaborative inquiry-action cycle, teachers become leaders in a group that "embraces certain collective obligations for student success and well-being that develops a certain collective expertise by employing problem-solving, critique, reflection, and debate" (Little, 2002, p. 46). The cycle harnesses the power of an inquiry-minded, action-oriented principal, teacher-leaders, committed parents, and invested community members. Real change for improvement results.

CHALLENGES TO COLLABORATIVE INQUIRY AND ACTION

Just getting people to collaborate is not easy. People resist change and new ideas; they avoid uncomfortable or conflictive situations. The inquiry-action cycle represents change and introduces diverse ideas with potential for conflict and disagreement. So people are likely to resist both the change and the collaboration of the cycle. Inquiry-minded, action-oriented principals recognize this; they don't blame people for what comes naturally. Instead, they anticipate resistance and create both incentives and an atmosphere that supports risk taking and constructive dissent. These principals remember that collaboration is the first step toward acceptance and ownership of the innovation that the cycle represents. They know that "if an innovation is imposed upon [people], without the chance to assimilate it to their experience, to argue it out, adapt it to their own interpretation with their working lives, they will do their best to fend it off" (Marris, 1974, p. 157). Authentic collaboration with inquiry and action itself creates zones that build will and capacity for change.

Furthermore, principals recognize that while teachers are often blamed for resisting, their resistance may be superficial. Deeper resistance often lies in the various communities related to the school, so principals must build will to collaborate among those outside the schoolhouse doors. To avoid resistance and build participation, the inquiry-minded, action-oriented principal works to create an environment that establishes the conditions for success. Rogers (2003) provided five characteristics for the diffusion of innovations:

1. Relative advantage—"the degree to which an innovation [the collaborative inquiry-action cycle] is perceived as better than the idea it supersedes" (p. 15)

2. Compatibility—"the degree to which an innovation [the collaborative inquiry-action cycle] is perceived as being consistent with the existing values, past experiences, and needs of potential adopters" (p. 15)

3. Complexity—"the degree to which an innovation [the collaborative inquiry-action cycle] is perceived as difficult to understand and use" (p. 16)

4. Trialability—"the degree to which an innovation [the collaborative inquiry-action cycle] may be experimented with on a limited basis" (p. 16)

5. Observability—"the degree to which the results of an innovation [the collaborative inquiry-action cycle] are visible to others" (p. 16)

Still, keeping the cycle going takes more than sheer will and capacity. Even the best inquiry-minded, action-oriented principals face challenges. To start and to keep the cycle going, principals must possess a profound awareness of context, in particular, the unique context of their school. They continually bring discourse back to the particulars of the setting and the problem, asking for consideration and reconsideration of what fits and why. They take on multiple roles: They maintain focus and facilitate the processes; they buffer against and bridge across environments. Inquiry-minded, action-oriented principals encourage and model flexibility, adapting and modifying the cycle as needed. They know that each cycle is unique, not only to each school but also to each problem.

CHAPTER SUMMARY

For too long, school reform has been marked by one product intervention after another (Whitehurst, 2009). Our collaborative inquiry-action cycle provides a more inclusive and meaningful process intervention that allows the school community to select the specific product interventions most needed. The cycle works because it brings together and gives voice to people from within and outside the schoolhouse. The framework provides a flexible and meaningful guide that can be adapted to fit the unique contexts of the school communities and the various problems of practice. With a tight focus on the core technology of schools—that is, teaching and learning—it is driven by practice—by what happens and can happen in the classroom. Participation in the cycle brings in what parents, citizens, businesses, agencies, and other groups in the community have to offer to support the learning of their young people. Often, the cost of change is not money, but commodities that people are more than willing to give: their time, ideas, and energy. And it keeps the eyes of the school community on the prize of improved instruction and increased student learning. In fact, cycles in operation in the school build momentum. As educators see practices implemented that positively impact student achievement, efficacy increases. In turn, they become more and more willing to participate. As parents and community members see the improvements, they become more willing to support and participate in the process itself. Ultimately, participation in the collaborative inquiry-action cycle means continuous learning for all in the school community.

As stewards of the public trust, principals have an ethical obligation to ensure that instruction in their schools prepares children equitably and with justice and care. If you are a principal or aspire to be a principal, no matter what your background, wherever you live and work, you can and should be inquiry-minded and action-oriented. Leading with the collaborative inquiry-action cycle can make it happen. You *can* do it—it is the right thing to do and leading with the collaborative inquiry-action cycle can help you make it happen.

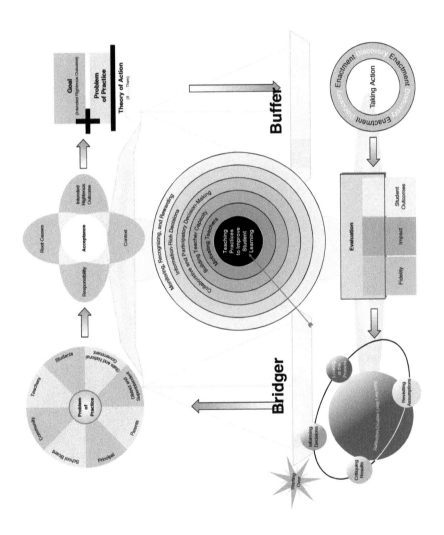

References

Abdal-Haag, I. (1998). *Professional development schools: Weighing the evidence.* Thousand Oaks, CA: Corwin.

Adler, L., & Gardner, S. (Eds.). (1994). *The politics of linking schools and social services.* Bristol, PA: Falmer.

Ainsworth, L. (2003). *Power standards: Identifying the standards that matter most.* Englewood, CO: Advanced Learning Press.

Amrein, A. L., & Berliner, D. C. (2002). High-stakes testing, uncertainty, and student learning. *Educational Policy Analysis Archives, 10*(18), Retrieved August 3, 2003, from http://epaa.asu.edu/epaa/v10n18/

Argyris, C., & Schon, D. (1974). *Theory in practice: Increasing professional effectiveness.* San Francisco: Jossey-Bass.

Ball, D., & Cohen, D. (1999). Developing practice, developing practitioners: Toward a practice-based theory of professional education. In L. Darling-Hammond & G. Sykes (Eds.), *Teaching as the learning profession* (pp. 3–32). San Francisco: Jossey-Bass.

Berman, P., & McLaughlin, M. W. (1978). *Federal programs supporting educational change: Implementing and sustaining innovation.* Santa Monica, CA: RAND.

Black, W. (2005, November 12). *A story of accountable talk: Contradictions and tension from the inside.* Paper presented at the University Council for Educational Administration, Nashville, TN.

Blase, J., & Blase, J. (1998). *Handbook of instructional leadership: How really good principals promote teaching and learning.* Thousand Oaks, CA: Corwin.

Bolman, L., & Deal, T. (2008). *Reframing organizations: Artistry, choice and leadership* (4th ed.). San Francisco: Jossey-Bass.

Bransford, J. P., Brown, A. L., & Cocking, R. R. (Eds.). (2000). *How people learn: Brain, mind, experience, and school.* Washington, DC: National Academic Press.

Brown, J. S., & Duguid, P. (2000). *The social life of information.* Boston: Harvard Business School Press.

Bryk, A. (2003). No Child Left Behind Chicago-style. In P. E. Peterson & M. West (Eds.), *No Child Left Behind? The politics and practice of school accountability* (pp. 242–262): Brookings Institution Press.

Carnoy, M., Loeb, S., & Smith, T. L. (2003). The impact of accountability policies in Texas high schools. In M. Carnoy, R. Elmore, & L. S. Siskin (Eds.), *The new accountability: High schools and high-stakes testing* (pp. 147–174). New York: RoutledgeFalmer.

Choo, C. W. (2001). The knowing organization as learning organization. *Education & Training, 43*(4/5), 197–205.

Christenson, S. L., & Sheridan, S. M. (2001). *School and families: Creating essential connections for learning.* New York: Gilford Press.

Chubb, J. E., & Moe, T. M. (1990). *Politics, markets, and America's schools.* Washington, DC: Brookings Institute.

Coburn, C., & Talbert, J. E. (2006). Conceptions of evidence use in school districts: Mapping the terrain. *American Journal of Education, 112*(4), 469–495.

Cohen, D. K. (1988). Teaching practice: Plus que ca change . . . In P. Jackson (Ed.), *Contributing to educational change: Perspectives on research and practice* (pp. 27–84). Berkeley, CA: McKutchen.

Cohen, D. K. (1990). A revolution in one classroom: The case of Mrs. Oublier. *Educational Evaluation and Policy Analysis, 12*(5), 311–329.

Crowson, R., & Boyd, W. L. (1993). Coordinated services for children: Designing arks for storms and sea unknown. *American Journal of Education, 101*(2), 140–179.

Daft, R. L., & Weick, K. E. (1984). Toward a model of organizations as interpretive systems. *Academy of Management Review, 9*(2), 284–295.

Darling-Hammond, L. (2004). Standards, accountability, and school reform. *Teachers College Record, 106*(6), 1047–1085.

Darling-Hammond, L., & Sykes, G. (Eds.). (1999). *Teaching as the learning profession: Handbook of policy and practice.* San Francisco: Jossey-Bass.

Davis, S., Darling-Hammond, L., LaPointe, M., & Meyerson, D. (2005). *School leadership study: Developing successful principals.* Stanford, CA: Stanford Educational Leadership Institute.

Day, C., Harris, A., Hadfield, M., Tolley, H., & Beresford, J. (2000). *Leading schools in times of change.* Buckingham, UK: Open University Press.

Deal, T. E., & Peterson, K. (1998). *Shaping school culture: The heart of leadership.* San Francisco: Jossey-Bass.

DiMaggio, P. J., & Powell, W. W. (1991). The iron cage revisited: Institutional isomorphism and collective rationality in organizational fields. In W. W. Powell & P. J. DiMaggio (Eds.), *The new institutionalism in organizational analysis* (pp. 63–82). Chicago: University of Chicago Press.

Driscoll, M. E. (2007). The circus animals' desertion: Lesson for leaders in the work of Philip W. Jackson. In D. T. Hansen, M. E. Driscoll, & R. V. Arcilla (Eds.), *A life in classrooms: Philip W. Jackson and the practice of education* (pp. 92–107). New York: Teachers College Press.

DuFour, R., Eaker, R., & DuFour, R. (Eds.). (2005). *On common ground: The power of professional learning communities.* Bloomington, IN: Solution Tree.

Earl, L., & Katz, S. (2002). Leading schools in a data-rich world. In K. Liethwood & P. Hallinger (Eds.), *Second international handbook of educational leadership and administration: Part two* (pp. 1003–1023). Dordrecht, The Netherlands: Kluwer Academic.

Earl, L., & Torrance, N. (2000). Embedding accountability and improvement into large-scale assessment: What difference does it make? *Peabody Journal of Education, 75*(4), 114–141.

Eberly, D. J. (1993). National youth service: A developing institution. *NASSP Bulletin, 77*(550), 50–57.

Elmore, R. (1979). Backward mapping: Implementation research and policy decisions. *Political Science Quarterly, 94*(4), 601–616.

Elmore, R. (1983). Complexity and control: What legislators and administrators can do about implementing public policy. In L. S. Shulman & G. Sykes (Eds.), *Handbook of teaching and educational policy* (pp. 342–369). New York: Longman.

Elmore, R. (2000). *Building a new structure for school leadership.* Washington, DC: Albert Shanker Institute.

Elmore, R. (2002a). *Bridging the gap between standards and achievement: The imperative for professional development in education.* Washington, DC: Albert Shanker Institute.

Elmore, R. (2002b). Hard questions about practice. *Educational Leadership, 59*(8), 22–25.

Elmore, R. (2003a). Accountability and capacity. In M. Carnoy, R. Elmore & L. S. Siskin (Eds.), *The new accountability: High schools and high-stakes testing* (pp. 195–209). New York: RoutledgeFalmer.

Elmore, R. (2003b). Conclusion: The problem of stakes in performance-based accountability systems. In S. H. Fuhrman & R. Elmore (Eds.), *Redesigning accountability systems for education* (pp. 274–296). New York: Teachers College Press.

Elmore, R., & Burney, D. (1999). Investing in teacher learning: Staff development and instructional improvement. In L. Darling-Hammond & G. Sykes (Eds.), *Teaching as the learning profession* (pp. 263–291). San Francisco: Jossey-Bass.

Elmore, R., Peterson, P. L., & McCarthy, S. (1996). *Restructuring in the classroom: Teaching, learning and school organization.* San Francisco: Jossey-Bass.

Epstein, J. (2001). *School, family, and community partnerships: Preparing educators and improving schools.* Boulder, CO: Westview Press.

Epstein, J., & Sanders, M. G. (2006). Prospects for change: Preparing educators for school, family, and community partnerships. *Peabody Journal of Education, 81*(2), 81–120.

Fink, D., & Brayman, C. (2006). School leadership succession and the challenges of change. *Educational Administration Quarterly, 42*(1), 62–89.

Firestone, W. (1996). Leadership roles or functions? In K. Leithwood, D. Chapman, P. Corson, P. Hallinger, & A. Hart (Eds.), *International handbook of educational leadership and administration* (pp. 395–418). Boston: Kluwer Academic.

Florida, R. (2002). *The rise of the creative class: And how it's transforming work, leisure, community and everyday life.* New York: Basic Books.

Forsyth, P. B., & Smith, T. O. (2002, April). *Patterns of principal retention: What the Missouri case tells us.* Paper presented at the American Educational Research Association, New Orleans, LA.

Friedman, T. (2007). *The world is flat 3.0: A brief history of the twenty-first century.* New York: Farrar, Straus and Giroux.

Fuhrman, S. H. (1999). *The new accountability* (No. Policy Brief 27). Philadelphia: Consortium for Policy Research in Education (CPRE).

Fullan, M. (1993). *Change forces.* Bristol, PA: Falmer Press.

Galbraith, J. A. (1977). *Organization design.* Reading, MA: Addison-Wesley.

Gamoran, A., & Grodsky, E. (2003). The relationship between professional development and professional community in American schools. *School Effectiveness and School Improvement, 14*(1), 1–29.

Goldring, E., & Hausman, C. S. (2001). Civic capacity and school principals: The missing links for community development. In R. Crowson (Ed.), *Community development and school reform* (pp. 193–209). Greenwich, CT: JAI Press.

Goldring, E., & Sullivan, A. (1996). Beyond the boundaries: Principals, parents and communities shaping the school environment. In K. Leithwood & J. Chapman (Eds.), *International handbook of educational leadership and administration* (pp. 195–222). Boston: Kluwer.

Goodlad, J. (1984). *A place called school: Prospects for the future.* New York: McGraw-Hill.

Hallinger, P., & Heck, R. (1996). Reassessing the principal's role in school effectiveness: A review of empirical research, 1980–1995. *Education Administration Quarterly, 32*(1), 5–44.

Halverson, R. (2003). Systems of practice: How leaders use artifacts to create professional community in schools. *Educational Policy Analysis Archives, 11*(37), 1–35.

Haney, W. (2000). The myth of the Texas miracle in education. *Educational Policy Analysis Archives, 8*(41). Retrieved January 12, 2001, from http://epaa.asu .edu/epaa/v8n2041/

Hawley, W., & Valli, L. (1999). The essentials of effective professional development: A new consensus. In L. Darling-Hammond & G. Sykes (Eds.), *Teaching as the learning profession: Handbook of policy and practice* (pp. 151–180). San Francisco: Jossey-Bass.

Hawley, W., & Valli, L. (2007). Design principles for learner-centered professional development. In W. Hawley & D. L. Rollie (Eds.), *The keys to effective schools: Educational reform as continuous improvement* (2nd ed., pp. 117–138). Thousand Oaks, CA: Corwin.

Henderson, A. T., Mapp, K. L., Johnson, V. R., & Davies, D. (2007). *Beyond the bake sale: The essential guide to family-school partnerships.* New York: New Press.

Hightower, A. (2002). San Diego's big boom: Systemic instructional change in the central office and schools. In A. Hightower, M. S. Knapp, J. A. Marsh, & M. W. McLaughlin (Eds.), *School districts and instructional renewal* (pp. 76–93). New York: Teachers College Press.

Homans, G. (1950). *The human group.* New York: Harcourt, Brace.

Hoover-Dempsey, K., & Sandler, H. M. (1997). Why do parents become involved in their children's education? *Review of Educational Research, 67*(1), 3–42.

Jones, B. D., & Egley, R. J. (2004). Voices from the frontlines: Teachers' perceptions of high-stakes testing. *Education Policy Analysis Archives, 12*(39). Retrieved May 28, 2005, from http://epaa.asu.edu/epaa/v12n39/

Joyce, B., & Showers, B. (1988). *Student achievement through staff development.* New York: Longman.

Kornhaber, M. L. (2004). Appropriate and inappropriate forms of testing, assessment, and accountability. *Educational Policy, 18*(1), 45–70.

Kotter, J. P. (1979). *Power in management.* New York: ANACOM.

Labaree, D. (1999). *How to succeed in school without really learning.* New Haven, CT: Yale University Press.

Lacireno-Paquet, N., Holyoke, T., Moser, M., & Henig, J. (2002). Creaming versus cropping: Charter school enrollment practices in response to market incentives. *Educational Evaluation and Policy Analysis, 24*(2), 145–158.

Lareau, A. (2000). *Home advantage: Social class and parental intervention in elementary education.* Lanham, MD: Rowman & Littlefield.

Leithwood, K., Jantzi, D., & Steinbeck, R. (1999). *Changing leadership for changing times.* Buckingham, UK: Open University Press.

Leithwood, K., & Mascall, B. (2008). Collective leadership effects on student achievement. *Educational Administration Quarterly, 44*(4), 529–561.

Leithwood, K., & Riehl, C. (2003). *What we know about successful school leadership. A report of Division A of AERA.* Washington, DC: American Educational Research Association.

Leithwood, K., Seashore Louis, K., Anderson, S., & Wahlstrom, K. (2005). *How leadership influences student learning.* New York: Wallace Foundation.

Leithwood, K., & Steinbach, R. (1991). Indicators of transformational leadership in the everyday problem solving of school administrators. *Journal of Personnel Evaluation in Education, 7*(4), 112–244.

Leithwood, K., & Wahlstrom, K. (2008). Linking leadership to student learning: Introduction. *Educational Administration Quarterly, 44*(4), 455–457.

Lemons, R., Luschei, T., & Siskin, L. S. (2003). Leadership and the demands of standards-based accountability. In M. Carnoy, R. Elmore, & L. S. Siskin (Eds.), *The new accountability: High schools and high-stakes testing* (pp. 99–128). New York: RoutledgeFalmer.

Lieberman, A., & Miller, L. (1999). *Teachers: Transforming their world and their work.* New York: Teachers College Press.

Lightfoot, S. L. (1983). *The good high school.* New York: Basic Books.

Little, J. W. (1982a). The effective principal. *American Education, 18,* 38–43.

Little, J. W. (1982b). Norms of collegiality and experimentation: Workplace conditions of school educators. *American Educational Research Journal, 19*(3), 325–340.

Little, J. W. (1993). Teachers' professional development in a climate of educational reform. *Educational Evaluation and Policy Analysis, 15*(2), 129–151.

Little, J. W. (2002). Professional communication and collaboration. In W. Hawley (Ed.), *The keys to effective schools: Educational reform as continuous improvement* (pp. 43–55). Thousand Oaks, CA: Corwin.

Lortie, D. (1975). *Schoolteacher.* Chicago: University of Chicago Press.

Louis, K. B., & Miles, M. B. (1990). *Improving the urban high school: What works and why.* New York: Teachers College Press.

Lubienski, C. (2006). School diversification in second-best education markets: International evidence and conflicting theories of change. *Educational Policy, 20*(2), 323–344.

Lutz, F., & Merz, C. (1992). *The politics of school/community relations.* New York: Teachers College Press.

Manswell Butty, J. L., LaPoint, V., Thomas, V. G., & Thompson, D. (2001). The changing face of after school programs: Advocating talent development for urban middle and high school students. *NASSP Bulletin, 85*(626), 22–34.

March, J. G. (1978). American public school administration: A short analysis. *School Review, 86*(2), 217–250.

March, J. G. (1999a). Exploration and exploitation in organizational learning. In J. G. March (Ed.), *The pursuit of organizational intelligence* (pp. 114–136). Malden, MA: Blackwell.

March, J. G. (1999b). Introduction. In J. G. March (Ed.), *The pursuit of organizational intelligence* (pp. 1–10). Malden, MA: Blackwell.

March, J. G. (1999c). Understanding how decisions happen in organizations. In J. G. March (Ed.), *The pursuit of organizational intelligence* (pp. 13–38). Malden, MA: Blackwell.

March, J. G., & Levinthal, D. (1999). The myopia of learning. In J. G. March (Ed.), *The pursuit of organizational learning* (pp. 193–222). Malden, MA: Blackwell.

March, J. G., & Simon, H. (1958). *Organizations*. New York: Wiley.

Marks, H. M., & Printy, S. M. (2003). Principal leadership and school performance: An integration of transformations and instructional leadership. *Educational Administration Quarterly, 39*(3), 370–397.

Marris, P. (1974). *Loss and change*. New York: Pantheon Books.

Marzano, R. J., Waters, T., & McNulty, B. (2005). *School leadership that works: From research to results*. Alexandria, VA: Association for Supervision and Curriculum Development.

Massell, D. (2001). The theory and practice of using data to build capacity: State and local strategies and their effects. In S. H. Fuhrman (Ed.), *From the capitol to the classroom: Standards-based reform in the states: One hundredth yearbook of the National Society for the Study of Education, Part II* (pp. 148–169). Chicago: University of Chicago Press.

Massell, D., & Goertz, M. E. (2002). District strategies for building instructional capacity. In A. M. Hightower, M. S. Knapp, J. A. Marsh & M. W. McLaughlin (Eds.), *School districts and instructional renewal* (pp. 43–60). New York: Teachers College Press.

Mawhinney, H. (1996). Institutional effects of strategic efforts at community enrichment. In W. J. Kritek & J. G. Cibulka (Eds.), *Coordination among schools, families, and communities: Prospects for educational reform* (pp. 223–243). Albany: State University of New York Press.

McLaughlin, M. W. (1990). The Rand change agent study: Ten years later. In A. Odden (Ed.), *Implementation* (pp. 143–155). New York: State University of New York Press.

McNeil, L. M. (2000). *Contradictions of reform: The educational costs of standardized testing*. New York: Routledge.

Merchant, B. M. (2004, April). *Tick, TAKS, toe—Fail and stay, pass and go: 3rd grade accountability, Texas style*. Paper presented at the annual meeting of the American Educational Research Association, San Diego, CA.

Meyer, J. W., & Rowan, B. (1991). Institutional organizations: Formal structure as myth and ceremony. In W. W. Powell & P. J. DiMaggio (Eds.), *The new institutionalism in organizational analysis* (pp. 41–82). Chicago: University of Chicago Press.

Militello, M., & Benham, M. (in press). "Sorting out" collective leadership: How Q-methodology can be used to evaluate leadership development. *Leadership Quarterly*.

Militello, M., Schweid, J., & Carey, J. C. (2008, March). *Si se puedes! How educators engage in open, collaborative systems of practice to affect college placement rates of low-income students*. Paper presented at the American Educational Research Association, New York City.

Militello, M., Sireci, S., & Schweid, J. (2008, March). *Intent, purpose, and fit: An examination of formative assessment systems in school districts*. Paper presented at the American Educational Research Association, New York City.

Mitgang, L. D. (2003). *Beyond the pipeline: Getting the principals we need, where they are needed most*. New York: Wallace Foundation.

Murphy, J. (2001). *The productive high-school: Creating personalized academic communications*. Thousand Oaks, CA: Corwin.

National Center for Educational Statistics. (2006). *The condition of education 2006* (No. NCES 2006–071). Washington, DC: U.S. Department of Education, Institute for Education Sciences.

National Center for Educational Statistics. (2008). *The condition of education 2008* (No. NCES 2008–032). Washington, DC: U.S. Department of Education, Institute for Education Sciences.

National Commission on Excellence. (1983). *A nation at risk: The imperative for educational reform* (No. GPO Publication No. 065-000-00177-2). Washington, DC: Government Printing Office.

Newmann, F., King, B., & Young, P. (2000, April). *Professional development that addresses school capacity: Lessons from urban elementary schools.* Paper presented at the annual meeting of the American Educational Research Association, New Orleans, LA.

Newmann, F., King, M. B., & Rigdon, M. (1997). Accountability and school performance: Implications from restructured schools. *Harvard Educational Review, 67*(1), 41–74.

O'Day, J. (2002). Complexity, accountability and school improvement. *Harvard Educational Review, 72*(3), 293–329.

Ogawa, R. T., Sandholtz, J., Martinez-Flores, M., & Scribner, S. P. (2003). The substantive and symbolic consequences of a district's standards-based curriculum. *American Educational Research Journal, 40*(1), 147–176.

Orfield, G. (2004a). *Dropouts in America: Confronting the graduation rate crisis.* Cambridge, MA: Harvard Education Press.

Orfield, G. (2004b). Introduction. In G. L. Sunderman & J. Kim (Eds.), *Inspiring vision, disappointing results: Four studies on implementing the No Child Left Behind Act* (pp. 1–10). Cambridge, MA: Harvard University, Civil Rights Project.

Orfield, G., & Lee, C. (2005). *Why segregation matters: Poverty and educational inequality.* Cambridge, MA: Harvard University, Civil Rights Project.

Pallas, A. M. (2001). Preparing education doctoral students for epistemological diversity. *Educational Researcher, 30*(5), 6–11.

Patton, M. Q. (1990). *Qualitative evaluation and research methods.* Newbury Park, CA: Sage.

Petrides, L. A., & Guiney, S. Z. (2002). Knowledge management for school leaders: An ecological framework for thinking schools. *Teachers College Record, 104*(8), 1702–1717.

Petrides, L. A., & Nodine, T. R. (2003). *Knowledge management in education: Defining the landscape.* Half Moon Bay, CA: Institute for the Study of Knowledge Management in Education.

Pfeffer, J., & Salancik, G. (1978). *The external control of organizations.* New York: Harper & Row.

Piaget, J. (1985). *The equilibrium of cognitive structures: The central problem of intellectual development* (T. Brown & K. J. Thampy, Trans.). Chicago: University of Chicago Press.

Pink, D. (2006). *A whole new mind: Why right-brainers will rule the future.* New York: Riverhead Books.

Popham, W. J. (2001). *The truth about testing: An educator's call to action.* Alexandria, VA: Association for Supervision and Curriculum Development.

Popham, W. J. (2004). Curriculum, instruction, and assessment: Amiable allies or phony friends? *Teacher College Record, 106*(3), 417–428.

Popham, W. J. (2008). *Transformative assessment.* Alexandria, VA: Association for Supervision and Curriculum Development.

Porter, A. C., Garet, M. S., Desimone, L., & Birman, B. (2003). Providing effective professional development: Lessons from the Eisenhower program. *Science Education, 12*(1), 23–40.

Pounder, D., Galvin, P., & Sheppard, P. (2003). An analysis of the United States educational administration shortage. *Australian Journal of Education, 47*(2), 133–145.

Pounder, D., Reitzug, U., & Young, M. (2002). Preparing school leaders for school improvement, social justice, and community. In J. Murphy (Ed.), *The educational leadership challenge: Redefining leadership for the 21st century* (pp. 261–288). Chicago: University of Chicago Press.

Printy, S. M. (2008). Leadership for teacher learning: A community of practice perspective. *Educational Administration Quarterly, 44*(2), 187–226.

Putnam, R. T., & Borko, H. (2000). What do new views of knowledge and thinking have to say about research on teacher learning? *Educational Researcher, 29*(1), 4–15.

Quinn, T. (2002). *Succession planning: Start today.* Retrieved February 12, 2007, from http://www.nassp.org

Rallis, S. F. (1990). Professional teachers and restructured schools: Leadership challenges. In B. Mitchell & L. L. Cunningham (Eds.), *Educational leadership and changing contexts of families, communities, and schools* (pp. 184–209). Chicago: University of Chicago Press.

Rallis, S. F., & Goldring, E. (2000). *Principals of dynamic schools: Taking charge of change* (2nd ed.). Thousand Oaks, CA: Corwin.

Rallis, S. F., & MacMullen, M. M. (2000). Inquiry minded schools: Opening doors for accountability. *Phi Delta Kappan, 81*(10), 766–773.

Rallis, S. F., Rossman, G. B., Cobb, C., Reagan, R. G., & Kuntz, A. (2008). *Leading dynamic schools: How to create and implement ethical policies.* Thousand Oaks, CA: Corwin.

Reeves, D. B. (2002). *Making standards work* (3rd ed.). Denver, CO: Advanced Learning Press.

Reeves, D. B. (2004). *Accountability for learning: How teachers and school leaders can take charge.* Alexandria, VA: Association for Supervision and Curriculum Development.

Robinson, V., Lloyd, C., & Rowe, K. (2008). The impact of leadership on student outcomes: An analysis of the different effects of leadership types. *Educational Administration Quarterly, 44*(5), 635–674.

Rogers, E. (2003). *Diffusion of innovation* (5th ed.). New York: Free Press.

Rosenholtz, S. J. (1989). *Teachers' workplace: The social organization of schools.* New York: Longman.

Rothstein, R. (2004). *Class and schools: Using social, economic, and educational reforms to close the black-white achievement gap.* New York: Teachers College Press.

Rowan, B. (1990). Commitment and control: Alternative strategies for the organizational design of schools. In C. B. Cazden (Ed.), *Review of research in education* (Vol. 16, pp. 353–389). Washington, DC: American Educational Research Association.

Roza, M., Celio, M., Harvey, J., & Wishon, S. (2003). *A matter of definition: Is there truly a shortage of school principals?* Washington, DC: Daniel J. Evans School of Public Affairs, Center on Reinventing Public Education.

Schmoker, M. (1999). *Results: The key to continuous school improvement* (2nd ed.). Alexandria, VA: Association for Supervision and Curriculum Development.

Schon, D. (1983). *The reflective practitioner.* New York: Basic Books.

Sebring, P., & Bryk, A. (2000). School leadership and the bottom line in Chicago. *Phi Delta Kappan, 81*(6), 440–443.

Senge, P. (1990). *The fifth discipline: The art and practice of the learning organization.* New York: Currency Doubleday.

Siskin, L. S. (2003). Outside the core: Accountability in tested and untested subjects. In M. Carnoy, R. Elmore, & L. S. Siskin (Eds.), *The new accountability: High schools and high-stakes testing* (pp. 87–98). New York: RoutledgeFalmer.

Sizer, T. (1992). *Horace's school: Redesigning the American high school.* New York: Houghton Mifflin.

Skrla, L., Scheurich, J. J., Johnson, J. F., & Koschoreck, J. W. (2004). Accountability for equity. Can state policy leverage social justice? In L. Skrla & J. J. Scheurich (Eds.), *Educational equity and accountability: Paradigms, policies, and politics* (pp. 51–78). New York: RoutledgeFalmer.

Smith, M. A., & O'Day, J. (1991). Systemic school reform. In S. H. Fuhrman & B. Malen (Eds.), *The politics of curriculum and testing* (pp. 233–267). New York: Falmer Press.

Smrekar, C. (1993, November). *The Kentucky Family Resource Centers: The leadership challenges of school-linked social services.* Paper presented at the Annual Convention of the University Council of Educational Administration, Houston, TX.

Spillane, J. (1999). External reform initiatives and teachers' efforts to reconstruct their practice: The mediating role of teachers' zone of enactment. *Journal of Curriculum Studies, 31*(2), 143–175.

Spillane, J. (2000). Cognition and policy implementation: District policymakers and the reform of mathematics education. *Cognition and Instruction, 18*(2), 141–179.

Spillane, J., Halverson, R., & Diamond, J. B. (2001). Investigating school leadership practice: A distributed perspective. *Educational Researcher, 30*(3), 23–28.

Spillane, J., Halverson, R., & Diamond, J. B. (2004). Toward a theory of leadership practice: A distributed perspective. *Journal of Curriculum Studies, 36*(1), 3–34.

Spillane, J., Reisner, B. J., & Reimer, T. (2002). Policy implementation and cognition. Reframing and refocusing implementation research. *Review of Educational Research, 72*(3), 387–431.

Stecher, B. (2002). Consequences of large scale, high stakes testing on school and classroom practice. In L. S. Hamilton, B. Stecher, & S. P. Klein (Eds.), *Making sense of test-based accountability in education* (pp. 79–100). Santa Monica, CA: RAND.

Stiggins, R. (2005). From formative assessment to assessment FOR learning: A path to success in standards-based schools. *Phi Delta Kappan, 87*(4), 324–328.

Supovitz, J. A. (2006). *The case for district-based reform: Leading, building, and sustaining school improvement.* Cambridge, MA: Harvard Education Press.

Supovitz, J. A., & Christman, J. B. (2003). *Developing communities of instructional practice: Lessons from Cincinnati and Philadelphia* (No. RB-39). Philadelphia, PA: Consortium for Policy Research in Education (CPRE).

Sykes, G. (1999). Teacher and student learning: Strengthening their connection. In L. Darling-Hammond & G. Sykes (Eds.), *Teaching as the learning profession: Handbook of policy and practice* (pp. 151–179). San Francisco: Jossey-Bass.

Sykes, G. (2002). Models of preparation for the professions: Implications for educational leadership. In M. S. Tucker & J. B. Codding (Eds.), *The principal challenge: Leading and managing schools in an era of accountability* (pp. 143–200). San Francisco: Jossey-Bass.

Sykes, G., & Elmore, R. (1988). Making schools manageable: Policy and administration for tomorrow's schools. In J. Hannaway & R. Crowson (Eds.), *The politics of reforming school administration: The 1988 yearbook of the Politics of Education Association* (pp. 77–94). New York: Falmer Press.

Thompson, J. (1967). *Organizations in action.* New York: McGraw-Hill.

Tyack, D., & Cuban, L. (1995). *Tinkering toward utopia: A century of public school reform.* Cambridge, MA: Harvard University Press.

U.S. Department of Education. (2002). *Strategic plan for 2002–2007* [Electronic Version]. Retrieved February 4, 2004, from http://www.ed.gov/about/reports/strat/plan2002–07/plan.pdf

U.S. Department of Education. (2003). *Using data to influence classroom decisions* [Electronic Version]. Retrieved July 28, 2007, from http://www.ed.gov/teachers/nclbguide/datadriven.pdf

Valencia, R. R., Valencia, A., Sloan, K., & Foley, D. E. (2004). Let's treat the cause, not the symptoms: Equity and accountability in Texas revisited. In L. Skrla & J. J. Scheurich (Eds.), *Educational equity and accountability: Paradigms, policies, and politics* (pp. 29–38). New York: RoutledgeFalmer.

Wahlstrom, K., & Seashore Louis, K. (2008). How teachers experience principal leadership: The roles of professional community, trust, efficacy, and shared responsibility. *Educational Administration Quarterly, 44*(4), 458–495.

Wayman, J., & Stringfield, S. (2006). Data use for school improvement: School practices and research perspectives. *American Journal of Education, 112*(4), 463–468.

Wehlage, G., Newmann, F., & Secada, W. A. (1996). Standards for authentic achievement and pedagogy. In F. Newmann & Associates (Eds.), *Authentic achievement: Restructuring schools for intellectual quality* (pp. 21–48). San Francisco: Jossey-Bass.

Weick, K. (1976). Educational organizations as loosely coupled systems. *Administrative Sciences Quarterly, 21*(1), 1–19.

Weiss, C. (1998). *Evaluation* (2nd ed.). Upper Saddle River, NJ: Prentice Hall.

Wenger, E. (1998). *Communities of practice: Learning, meaning and identity.* Cambridge, NY: Cambridge University Press.

Wenger, E. (1999). Communities of practice and social learning systems. *Organization, 7*(2), 225–246.

Whitehurst, G. (2009). *Innovation, motherhood, and apple pie.* Brown Center on Education Policy. Washington, DC: The Brookings Institution.

Wiggins, G. (1996). Embracing accountability. *New Schools, New Communities, 12*(2), 4–10.

Wiggins, G., & McTighe, J. (2005). *Understanding by design* (2nd ed.). Upper Saddle River, NJ: Prentice Hall.

Wilson, S., & Berne, J. (1999). Teacher learning and the acquisition of professional knowledge: A review of research on contemporary professional development. In Iran-Nejad & P. D. Pearson (Eds.), *Review of research in education* (Vol. 24, pp. 173–209). Washington, DC: American Educational Research Association.

Young, V. M. (2006). Teachers' use of data: Loose coupling, agenda setting, and team norms. *American Journal of Education, 112*(4), 521–548.

Index

CORWIN

A SAGE Company

The Corwin logo—a raven striding across an open book—represents the union of courage and learning. Corwin is committed to improving education for all learners by publishing books and other professional development resources for those serving the field of PreK–12 education. By providing practical, hands-on materials, Corwin continues to carry out the promise of its motto: **"Helping Educators Do Their Work Better."**

Printed in the USA
CPSIA information can be obtained
at www.ICGtesting.com
JSHW050719041023
49619JS00019B/173